# THE BLACKPILL THEORY

why incels are right & you are wrong.

# THE BLACKPILL THEORY

why incels are right & you are wrong.

*Dr. Lukas Castle*

# INTRODUCTION

This book takes readers on a tour of the increasingly predictable explanations behind the lack of intimacy and affection suffered by a growing subset of young men today.

I have committed the last ten years of my life to the study of men who struggle to find intimacy, both sexually and emotionally. This process has involved assessing male psychologies and sexual behaviors, reconsidering mainstream beliefs, and meeting men who have had unfortunate experiences in this arena. The information collected through this effort will be revealed in the following pages.

As a trained ethnographer with a Ph.D. in the social sciences, my past academic scholarship has focused on male body image dissatisfaction, and masculinities[1].

I only offer these credentials because the following subject material is often easily dismissed in our wider culture and I believe that it should no longer be; a clear and studied analysis of the "incel" and "blackpill" phenomena can create a more nuanced cultural understanding of those involved in these subcultures, and perhaps of masculinity in general. To my knowledge, there is no published work which offers a fully elaborative point of view of human sexuality from the perspective of those who do not experience human sexuality.

By approaching these topics from an analytical standpoint and with scientific data, I hope this text can inspire closer and more sincere study of these issues.

Although academic sources are used throughout the book, the purpose is not to offer a scholastic text. I have tried to write in non-technical language that can be understood by readers from all backgrounds. I mainly want to share this book with involuntary celibates (incels), but I hope that all readers will patiently consider the data and arguments presented below.

Part of my motivation for pouring so much energy into this area of study comes from my own personal disillusionment with the current climate of academia.

Another part, the bigger one, comes from interviews I conducted with young men, mostly centering on their lack of sexual experiences as college students. Oftentimes, these interviews brought the interviewees to tears. In these charged interactions, I realized I was about to tumble down a rabbit hole of surprising information.

This journey started for me in 2009. Dating apps like Tinder weren't around yet. Seeking romance online was still generally stigmatized. Incel slang was not a thing. Social media was in its infancy and most romantic relationships still began organically "in real life."

In those days, my primary concerns were fulfilling the requirements of my master's degree and choosing which happy hour my graduate cohort would attend each Thursday night. During one of these happy hour excursions, the discussion shifted towards the lack of sexual and emotional intimacy faced by some guys in the group.

This was one of my first open conversations about the reality of the evolving sexual marketplace and male social isolation.

We all seemed to notice a genuine change in women's mating preferences, but we still weren't exactly sure of the standards needed to be met? In other words, both our social and romantic roles, as men, were lined with confusion. Centuries ago, a man's primary role was to provide and protect. Now? We weren't quite sure. Our roles were no longer defined and none of us could agree upon a clear model of what it meant to be considered "an attractive man."

Something was certainly off but of my peers, I was one of the first who emphasized the significance of an attractive outwardly appearance. When it came to improving the possibilities of developing intimate relationships with women, I knew that looks *did* matter.

This awareness shaped my own habits. I lifted weights, ate well, bought a lot of unnecessary dietary supplements, and curated a stylish wardrobe for myself. Over time, I began to observe that more and more men were spending time at the gym and dressing in higher fashion. My own personal habits seemed to be gaining more and more popularity in our culture. My school's weight room, empty just a few years prior, became crowded with young men. What was the motivation behind this sudden male desire to lift weights?

That question was the focal point of my master's thesis.

As an amateur academic, my research plan was not sophisticated. But the interviews I conducted with sexless, college-aged men is where the real journey began.

---

### WHAT IS THE BOOK ABOUT?

---

Humans today are free to pursue as many sexual experiences as we desire, with little risk to our health and safety. But not everyone gets approved for this basic human need (see Chapter IV, The Importance of Sex).

What emerges below is a portrait of the unlucky men who are left out of the mating market. The ramifications of their unmet sexual and emotional needs will be showcased in hopes that society can overcome some of its biases against these men.

The unintended consequences of how people meet and evaluate each other, especially those resulting from recent shifts in dating dynamics, will be demonstrated intensely.

The conclusions below are drawn from biological determinism, sociology, sociobiology, evolutionary psychology, and the refutation of the "just-world fallacy."

I have spent many hours observing online male forums. Sometimes I have actively participated in these online discussions, but mostly I have observed thousands of anecdotes posted by anonymous users. This type of non-participant observational methodology is termed a "netnography"[2]: an account of what transpires online.

Combined, all of this information will present a theory of social interaction which has come to be known as the blackpill.

With an understanding of the "blackpilled" point of view, the reader will be able to both explain and predict outcomes in many social and dating interactions.

Yes, it is that powerful.

With that said, the science in this text is generally considered taboo or will be considered "toxic." I foresee that most people will deny the evidence being presented here. The truth often makes us feel uncomfortable, and that is partly why blackpill thinking is avoided by so many.

But in a society built upon lies, all truths are considered toxic. Consider this as you read.

I am fully aware that the blackpill thinking can form a slippery slope to dark and nihilistic thinking. While my aim is to show how blackpill thought is, in many ways, in line with reality, I do not aim to endorse its extremist nihilistic conclusions.

Whatever merits these beliefs might have, please remember that the ideology as a whole is ultimately evolutionarily maladaptive and socially unproductive.

Blackpill ideology guarantees no positive outcome, especially for the incel. Whatever truths the blackpill ideology may contain, it is still at odds with the laws of the social world. It is therefore a theory that is difficult to put into practice.

Incels are the primary intended audience of this book – young men under the age of 35 who want to feel like "normal" human beings, and who believe that their lack of access to sexual and emotional intimacy dooms them to be eternal outcasts. In other words, they believe they cannot access affection and love, and they blame this on women and society as a whole.

I draw upon several sources to explain why this group of people struggle to attain these basic human needs.

From following online incel communities, I conclude that the majority of these guys are likeable, but have been thrown some very unfortunate punches.

Some are born into poverty, others are born without attractive physical qualities, some have psychiatric conditions like autism, and some have the misfortune of all of these at once. Some do not have the resolve to get up from every punch life throws them, and decide that the only solution is to stop fighting altogether.

Other incels find it easier to blame their misfortunes on something or someone else (i.e. "all women are hypergamous sluts"), instead of pursuing self-improvement. Almost all struggle to find a place in life and cope with their sense of marginalization.

I ask the reader to try to empathize with incels, just as you would empathize with other marginalized groups.

Popular consciousness focuses on the extremist tendencies of the incel movement. I hope this book will help outline the underlying causes for those excesses and incite a more humanist view.

Like anyone else, incels long for a more compassionate, supportive society, and want to live in a world where understanding comes second nature.

Feelings of self-doubt are not just a men's issue. Suicidal thoughts, severe depression, and rates of self-injury among all American college students more than doubled in less than a decade[3]. For millennials in particular, depression is on the rise – this is primarily linked to issues such as loneliness and money stress.

With all of that noted, we are often led to believe that the truth equals hate – and that is not accurate. The truth is truth and hate is hate.

The truth is that the sky is blue, but we do not hate that the sky is blue, just as we do not hate the grass for being green. When women's mating preferences are discussed in the book, there is no element of hate attached to those observable tendencies. They are what they are and should be accepted by all men.

With all that acknowledged, is there a notable degree of *hate* against women, particularly among incel online populations? Absolutely. Are these same incels misogynistic? Certainly.

The goal here is not to provide any justification for the hatred and toxicity embedded in aspects of the incel subculture. The hateful and misogynistic excesses that have come to define this ideology must be roundly condemned.

At the same time, academia must make a sincere inquiry into the world which created the incel phenomenon and professed "blackpill" thinking.

From the perspective of the incel, his animosity or frustrations toward others exists because of the rejections he faces every single day, for factors outside of his control. What are these rejections rooted in? What social and biological factors contribute to these rejections?

This experience of rejection, more than hateful rhetoric or activity, is what defines and galvanizes the incel community. The majority of these guys are just looking for a like-minded online forum to vent about their frustrations with life, loneliness, and women.

There is a spectrum within this community — not all these guys subscribe to a hateful anti-female rhetoric. Sharing these experiences can provide catharsis and peace. It is cathartic to know that there are others in comparable situations, feeling the same emotions. And for those who do hate, we will unpack why this sentiment exists, and what, if anything, can be done about it.

Some readers will be in great appreciation of the blackpill. For them the dots will connect very predictably, creating a logical final picture. For others, it will not be as easily digested. Consuming this information can be life-changing. It can also be soul-crushing.

---

## A WARNING TO INCEL READERS

---

The blackpill might be liberating, but it comes at the price of the loss of comfort and naiveté, of happy innocence. Harsh truths are cold and unforgiving, and blackpill thought is full of harsh truths.

Even if this something you do not wish were true, one needs to accept that the universe does not run on wishes and hopes. The blackpill is exhausting. It's pervasive. It's draining. It's unfortunate.

Reading this book is not going to be an enjoyable experience.

The blackpill isn't just "you do not have a girlfriend because you are ugly." Although, that is an aspect of the blackpill, the theory goes much further than that. It is complex and multifaceted.

For an incelibate man, the blackpill is a lens that can be directed toward everything in his life, and which brings all confusion in crystal-clear focus. The theory explains the struggle with online dating, why certain physical traits are rewarded and why others are punished, and why feelings of hopelessness or suicide are common.

This information might provide comfort for some, but for others, it will be mentally damaging – it will suffocate your mind.

Interpretation of the blackpill will lead to the conclusion that unless one is willing to overcome insurmountable odds, he will never experience a romantic relationship or achieve any value, at all.

To be blunt, the blackpill is a road to the bottom. It concludes that things will never get better.

Once an individual adopts this ideology, his life takes on a whole new veneer. Even typical mundane social interaction will suddenly pulse with dark new meaning; the unfortunate side effect is that this mundane conversation, which once seemed ordinary, now will seem sinister.

Nearly every interaction and nearly every form of entertainment, will be underlined by a blackpill perspective. Re-watching your favorite movies will lead to alternative interpretations. Familiar songs will become frustrating to listen to.

Most of all, one will judge people – especially couples – with more scrutiny, observing how they speak, behave, and interact together. A simple walk through the local mall or grocery store will, at times, be barely tolerable.

*Why did that happen? Why did he talk to me in that way? Why is she behaving like that? Do I deserve to be treated like this? What did I do? If I was over six feet tall, would that have happened? And: That couple does not really love each other. That lyric makes me sick to my stomach. I hate this movie now.* And so on.

The blackpill will open a third eye which can never be closed. There will be a whispering voice in your mind that will never stay quiet.

After reading this book, one of the most frustrating aspects is that you will suddenly understand perfectly why your situation is a problem… but you will not be able to solve it.

Some locks just do not have a key.

There are a number of diseases like this where we know pretty much exactly what causes it and how it progresses, yet there is no cure. Sometimes you are just screwed, even with a perfect understanding of the issue.

# I. UNDERSTANDING THE INCEL PROBLEM

Romantic dissatisfaction is one of the biggest issues we face in our society. This affects self-identifying incels, but it also impacts almost everyone else.

Roughly one third of the male population is currently sexless or incel. [4] This is a record high.

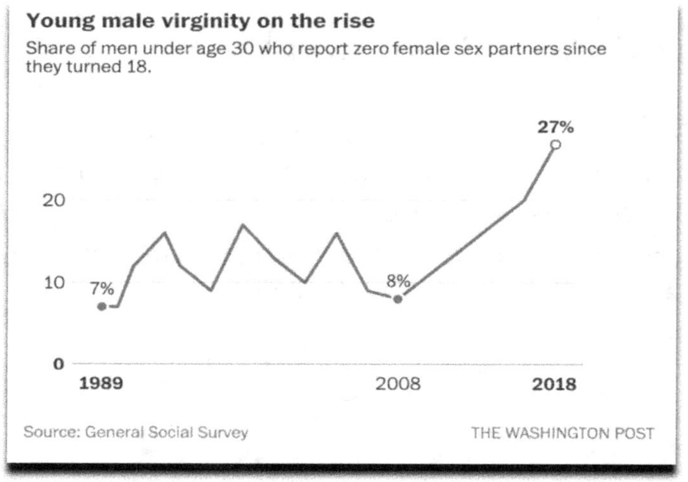


Sex is important for a healthy human psyche, and most of these affected men are still in their twenties with developing psychologies. It will be interesting to observe how things progress as sexless men turn 30 and above.

Simply telling the sexless men – incels – to "be better" just isn't good enough. It simply doesn't make sense to treat this problem, which has unstudied psychological complexity, with this approach. We do not tell the schizophrenic to "try harder." We accept that they have a pathology, and try to treat it clinically.

We need to find an effective way to tackle a very complex issue, which we are only just beginning to collect information from. We also need to create a more useful rhetoric than the one currently used regarding incels.

The first step is acknowledging that inceldom is ingrained in certain oppressive cultural and economic factors (namely, beauty standards and classism) that engender inequality throughout our society. These factors contribute to the pervasive suffering for incel men, not only in the United States, but throughout the world. As sociologists would explain it, increasing rates of inceldom in society are indicative of a veritable social problem.

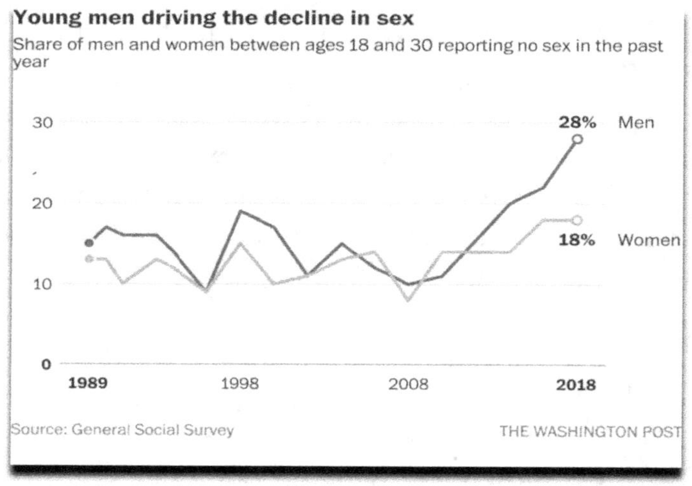


Before continuing with the unfortunate realities and societal projections of this potential crisis[5], it is necessary to clarify the incel situation.

Truthful and accurate definitions are important because of the unfortunate and pervasive mischaracterization of the way 'incels' are portrayed in the media.

## ACCURATE MEANING OF INCEL

Incel stands for "involuntary celibate."[6]

These are individuals who do not have sex, regardless of how much they might want to, as opposed to others who simply chose to refrain from intercourse (voluntary celibates).

Incels are a group of people, usually male, who are physically unattractive and because of this they believe their struggles with the opposite sex are for reasons beyond their control.

An incel desires more than just sex. Emotional intimacy and companionship are both core needs of the group (just as they are for non-incels).

Sex is just the most blatant form of intimacy, so it's often the primary focus when people discuss incel "subcultures".

# THE MISCHARACTERIZATION OF THE WORD INCEL

Despite what is written in mainstream media, being an 'incel' is not an ideology or a social movement, it is simply a state of being.

The actual meaning of the word has lost all original interpretation. The term "incel" is thrown around in all kinds of discussions and it has come to be used as a shaming device for any commentary which might be perceived as sexist or hateful towards women (regardless if the comment actually is offensive or not).

For example, if I say, "women have preferences for men over six feet tall," this could be interpreted as, "misogynistic." The stock dismissal comeback to this "hateful" statement, then, is simply, "found the incel!"

We see this play out like clockwork across our current culture – even in discussions that do not even remotely involve incels. The topics of sex and sexuality are so charged that conversations often devolve into these accusatory screaming matches.

But when questioned about the actual meaning of the word, the user will claim that they are not attacking the sexual failure or the masculinity or the virginity of male incels, but rather hatred for the opposite sex. In other words, they are using the word incorrectly, to mean something it does not.

We already have a term for hatred towards women: "misogynist." Right?

Shockingly, despite this word restructuring, we never observe them crying phrases such as "found the misogynist!" or "who hurt you misogynist!?"

Unless these weirdos just simply like to change the meanings of traditional words because they are unable to compete in the marketplace of ideas or debate properly. Which is, of course, a strong possibility.

The other possibility, a very revealing one, is that the users of the word "incel" recognize that the established term for hateful views toward women, "misogynist," is just not a sufficient insult — even though it is the most accurate.

Why might this be? People concede, subconsciously, that there just is not enough humiliation attached to being branded as a "misogynist." Because the blackpilled truth is that tall and handsome "misogynists" can still be successful with women.

It is possible that reckless users of the term "incel" know this subconsciously. And as such, they understand that the word "misogynist" does not hit hard enough.

If humiliation and shame are the goal, using the word "incel" as a tactical insult has now become common practice. This is because the word 'misogynist' fails to deliver the potent attack toward a man's sexual failure, which the word, "incel," accomplishes.

The insulted in connotation of "incel," as it is used today, derives from much deeper human tendencies.

In a patriarchal society such as ours, a man who does not have sexual relationships will be considered a pathetic loser. On this basis, having zero sexual or reproductive success has become an acceptable focus of ridicule.

In today's society, the incel bears the brunt of this ridicule. He has become the focus, the clear modern target, for an age-old ridicule rooted in the deep foundations of our society. This is basically the raw rule of nature expressing itself through the mouths of modern humans.

But beyond all this, in any arena where perspective is challenged by opponents and scrutinized by third-party onlookers, factual arguments must be the main weapon, not shaming tactics.

Despite their unfortunate approach to discussion, incels still envy normal people (whom they call "normies[7]") because these regular looking individuals do get to enjoy relationships and other forms of intimacy. The incels failure to secure similar emotions makes them feel like social rejects.

So, the abuse of the word "incel" as a shaming tactic throws salt into a wound. It only makes incels more depressed and more resentful. It confirms their darkest fears about rejection from "normie" society. It confirms that the "normies" see them as inhuman and monstrous.

With this all acknowledged, many incels exhibit misogynistic traits. And many incels blame the opposite sex for their plight. The productive response to the hatred across the incel community is not to shame but to understand.

## DISMISSING CRITICS – THE BIGGEST INCEL MISCONCEPTIONS

The negative reactions to this book will be all too similar. Distractors will openly state that "incels just need to suck it up " or that "life isn't fair" or that "they will never support racist, misogynistic pigs." It would be naïve to anticipate anything less.

These same people will acknowledge individuals born into poverty will be likely to stay poor throughout their entire life course. These same people will admit that race grants some individuals privilege, while leaving others at a disadvantage.

They will admit rich people have superior lives overall because they can afford better schools for their children and access to quality healthcare, among other things.

They have no issues understanding that some inborn circumstances handicap people, for their entire lives. But when it comes to DATING? Full stop – the human experience suddenly becomes just and fair! There is absolutely zero chance it could be affected by factors beyond your control!

You are an adult male virgin incel because you don't make enough money, you're out of shape, eat poorly, and don't have any social graces. Simple as that! All these hard-luck circumstances, which these critics would sympathize with in any other context, are levelled against the incel as attacks. *It's always his fault.*

Why do we assume this one aspect of our lives, dating and sex, is always controllable? That if we put effort into romance and bettering ourselves, no matter how short or ugly the starting point, we will *always* be rewarded with a caring, loving relationship?

It is almost as if people are frightened to acknowledge they do not have as much control over their dating prospects as they believe they do.

Incels are not 'incel' because they hate women, just as the wind is not blowing because the trees are shaking or having a low-self-esteem causes you to be bullied. Most of the time, despite fringe cases, kids get bullied due to their physical appearances and then develop low-self-esteem as a result. Likewise, some incels begin to hate women because of their lack of successes with them - because of their negative real-life experiences or absence thereof. Not because of some inborn misogyny.

These guys are not born with this hate, we can assume, just as Bobby Joe from Alabama is not born racist – clearly personal experience and social conditions have influenced them to adopt these inhumane and hateful perspectives.

Unfortunately, once the negative mentality begins, it spirals downward. The hatefulness that consumes incels gets more and more difficult for many of them to let go of – they become bitter and angry and even want to give completely up with life.

The media has never really attempted to humanize these individuals, to understand their predicament, or to place themselves into the shoes of sexless young men. Every single one of us learned about this approach to humanity during our freshmen year Introduction to Sociology course – it is called using a sociological imagination.

Take a second and wonder what it would be like to constantly feel unwanted. Imagine yourself as a fly on the wall in the incel world. Observe the world from a distance, consider it as a strange play. And remember you are but the audience in this play.

Observe what it would be like to never get a phone notification.

To never have someone compliment you. To routinely feel like you are an outsider. To never have a hug or a kiss. To miss out on homecoming or prom. To look in the mirror and feel disgusted every time.

The loneliness and sadness just compounds upon itself.

And all of these bleak emotional experiences are because of factors outside of your control. Your bones just did not properly align in the manner widely considered to be "attractive." Depressing.

Anyways, below are the eight most common misconceptions surrounding inceldom. Breaking each down will help streamline the above points.

---

### 1. "INCELS ARE INCEL BECAUSE THEY ONLY WANT TO DATE HOT, SUCCESSFUL WOMEN."

---

Where did this idea even come from? The notion that incels have these abnormally high standards of rejecting ugly women is such a wind up. Understand this once more: many incels have never even had a single opportunity to ever reject a woman. Ever.

Instead, the problem is that they do not even know what it is like to receive *any* sexual attention.

A young man does not suddenly "become" an incel. He goes through adolescence and determines, after years have passed, that others do not find him physically attractive, then he might reach the conclusion on his own accord.

Overwhelmingly incels (and men in general[8]) want to date someone they consider to be their "looksmatch."

A "looksmatch" is simply someone from the opposite sex who is in an equal relative tier of the incel's own attractiveness (e.g. a 3/10 man and a 3/10 woman, would be considered a perfect looksmatch). Women are generally matching with someone more attractive than themselves; men are generally matching with someone less attractive than themselves.

We see this type of selection process play out over and over on dating apps, which just so happen to be the most popular means to find a mate in 2019 (see Chapter VI, Dating Apps).

Observe the bar charts[9] on the next page, from the since deleted OkCupid blog research, which demonstrates women rate ~80% of men physically below average, while the men's ratings are more normally distributed.

Christian Rudder, the guy who founded OkCupid, published his sites secret data about dating; he is apparently not shy about presenting unflattering information and even wrote a book about it.

This trend where women are more selective than men in picking their matches also manifests on newer apps such as Tinder[10] and Hinge.[11]

The Tinder study does not expand much on which metrics were used to define selectivity so we can only assume this relates to factors such as education level, success, and physical appearance. However, one of the highlights indicated that men who were more educated than the women, were nearly twice as likely to receive a match.

Conversely, men do not show a preference or an aversion to highly educated women on Tinder; men primarily appear to be indifferent to the woman's education when choosing partners.

In sum, the problem is not because incels want someone exceptionally more attractive or successful than they are. To the contrary: it is actually women who are the more selective gender[12] (which makes sense evolutively speaking).

And since women are pickier about their mating choices, the men at the bottom of the stack are being left behind.

## 2. "INCELS BELIEVE THEY ARE ENTITLED TO SEX."

Nope – this is just an easy way to demonize incels for an overly simplistic interpretation of entitlement.

Incels are entitled to a sexual drive – just as any non-incel is. But they are not out in public ordering women to drop their pants.

Incels are just frustrated that women do not find them sexually attractive enough to want to sleep with them. This frustration expands far beyond the realm of sex. Overwhelmingly, incels just want a normal life, nothing special, just to be able to partake in dating, and intimacy, and love, and hopefully, have a family someday.

After years and years of rejection, unfortunately, many do not even see a strategy to activate a path to this basic life model.

The act of sex is an indispensable part of the intimacy that incels want, but it is still just one aspect of several. To cuddle; to kiss; to hold and be held; to look someone in the eyes and see that she wants to be with you: these features of a standard relationship are all part of the intimacy that incels desire. Of course, once that variety of affection and intimacy is established, sex often follows naturally.

If intimacy were a mountain, sex would just be the ice-covered peak – and incels do not just want to plant the flag on the summit they want to climb that whole damned thing.

Moreover, we need to stop pretending that, solitary "sex" (masturbation), is *real* sex. Digital pornography cannot mimic the expressiveness of an actual intimate sexual outing with a willing partner. This claim, alongside the claim that, "greater sexual access is no longer just the purview of the most attractive, the wealthiest, the most discreet, or the biggest risk-takers"[13] are both patently absurd.

This is not a preference of lingo, it is just reality. Sex is sex. Sitting in your bedroom, lonely and dejected, binging nightly on digital pornography, while fantasizing about an actual companion who would never consider you as a romantic prospect is sad and depressing. Masturbating is not and should not be considered as a permanent, lifetime replacement for a real-life, willing partner.

Sure, masturbation has its benefits, but not when it is your *only* source of intimacy or sexual behavior. It is a substitute.[14]

The reason why incels (and non-incels) want intimacy is quite simple — humans have both an instinctive drive to want sex, and a remarkably deep-seated need for being touched in a benign way. For incels, these very strict biological demands are remaining unfulfilled.

One incel confesses to other members of the online community:

> "The only extended physical contact I've received in recent memory was when I had my annual mental breakdown a month or so back, and I was sitting there sobbing like a bitch, so my mother and father came over and just gave me a hug while I cried. For a little while afterwards it was like 30 years of this crushingly immense amount of pain and stress and anger was temporarily lifted off my shoulders for a few precious

minutes. I can't even begin to imagine how much healthier and happier I'd be if I experienced that on a regular basis."

It is strange how a public misunderstanding of incels created this illogical leap that sexless men – who desires intimacy, and who want to be physically or emotionally valued – would feel entitled to commit physical assault or rape. Not only are these acts reprehensible and illegal – they are acts that most incelibate men would be mentally, emotionally, and probably physically incapable of performing.

The rationality just is not there. Sexual assault and rape are the literal opposite of wanting to feel loved or desired. Conceptually, these are two inherently opposing and incompatible concepts. Wanting to feel desired or appreciated necessitates that someone places value into you, which means that no force or coercion of any kind can or should be involved.

Of course, desiring love, intimacy, and sex are natural – especially when those needs have been unmet for extended periods, if not your entire life.

We must look at incels, in general, as people with extremely common and normal desires – not as would-be criminals wanting to commit heinous, abusive, and violent acts.

It is totally understandable to feel a sense of loss, regret, or even resentment for opportunities lost and needs left unfulfilled during arguably the prime years of one's life (not just in terms of physicality but also circumstance). These are normal and reasonable feelings.

It is shocking to observe people who are in a position of privilege regarding attractiveness (we will later discuss how attractiveness empowers and privileges people in nearly every arena of life) could so carelessly and easily flaunt that advantage and use it as a tool to shame, vilify, and delegitimize unattractive men. At the very least, we should be able to expect some level of self-awareness and humility.

The precise reasons why incels cannot fulfill this need for intimacy varies on a case by case basis. And it is almost always a combination of varied factors.

The potential limiting factors are described in further detail in Chapter V – What Women Find Attractive.

---

### 3. "INCELS ARE INCELS BECAUSE THEY ARE NOT TRYING HARD ENOUGH AND HAVE BAD PERSONALITIES."

---

One recurring theme is that outsiders usually assume that incels are just not trying.

The "just try harder" and "improve yourself" suggestions are all predicated on the belief that if an incel puts in the right amount of effort, he will procure the appropriate reward.

The majority of people refuse to admit that some people are so ugly that overcoming that physical impression is all but impossible. If a guy is extremely short, or bald, or facially ugly these physical traits can override even the most drastic material or economic improvements. Even physical fitness has a ceiling of improvement which is contingent on the starting point.

Devotion to a fitness regime is still valuable for the mental health aspect, but there is only so much one can change externally if he is just a meager 5'5" tall, with a small frame, bad muscle insertions, while also balding and facially deformed.

Unfortunately, these immutable traits are just not negligible. They matter more than any degree of muscle mass manufactured inside the gym.

Overall, many guys *do* put in effort – they buy stylish wardrobes, get regular haircuts, are well-groomed, take showers, chain watch YouTube videos to learn how to talk to girls, have degrees and jobs, own vehicles and homes, and are willing to get into serious relationships. But after all these enhancements or personality improvements, it is still a struggle.

Psychological disadvantages are also a major contributor to involuntary celibacy.

Like physical unattractiveness, pre-existing mental disabilities are hurdles that the majority of observers often overlook when judging incels from a normative perspective. Some incels are incels because of mental conditions that they cannot fix by "trying harder."

For example, only 32.1% of people with autism spectrum disorder (ASD) ever had a partner, while only 9% were married[15] (about half of all United States adults are married).

Another sample with an average age of diagnosis of 36 years old found that 44.6% of autistic men are still virgins, and only 16% are in a relationship.[16] This type of personality disorder makes it challenging to create meaningful bonds with people; having a normal life and relationships is incredibly difficult.

Therefore, beyond the looks component of the mating market, psychological issues can absolutely be the main reason for inceldom and a lack of social confidence.

If society as a whole recognized how being both neurotypical and attractive gives you a leg up over the autistic and unattractive, that would be a good start, in beginning to meet the problem of inceldom on its own terms.

Because if a man is unattractive enough, or has communication issues, or scores high on the autism spectrum, the chances of finding a relationship are minimal.

It should come as no surprise then that autism is a pervasive problem among incels. In an October 2019, survey administered on incels.co, 25.9% of the total participants indicated that they suffer from autism.[17]

This is all explained in more detail later on in the book.

---

## 4. "INCELS JUST NEED TO HIRE HOOKERS AND STOP COMPLAINING."

---

In order to create a useful rhetoric for this complicated situation, we must stop regarding sex work as a magical panacea to cure inceldom. We also must stop ignoring the fact that incels are interested in more than just the sexual aspect of a romantic relationship.

It was almost a weekly occurrence that an incel would vent to the online community that he was given the advice to "just get a hooker, dude!" The typical "sex-having" person does not understand and struggles to comprehend the core problem here.

Incels are not just sex-starved, they are starved of all forms of affection and intimacy. Incels fantasize about having a relationship – a girlfriend –  and creating a deep, meaningful bond with her.

Being a *fuckboi* who just pumps and dumps as many women as possible is not even on the radar of the typical incelibate man.

Further, being an incel is not exclusively about sexual exclusion – it is also about social exclusion. Many of these guys have endured stretches of life that could be defined as psychologically debilitating isolation resulting from intentional social exclusion and bullying.

Incels with these conditions need healthy structure in life that can improve their mental health and well-being.

Hiring a sex worker is simply not a remedy for the incels wide-ranging sense of isolation and exclusions.

---

### 5. "INCELS ARE A CULT OR A SOCIAL MOVEMENT."

---

The inability to get laid is an objective fact and is distinct from (and does not require) identification with the incel label.

Being an incel is not an ideology, it is a description of a condition. Once again, it simply refers to men who despite wanting to, cannot get laid.

Incels may or may not identify as incel.

Just as someone may recognize that their face does not meet cultural beauty standards without identifying as an "ugly" person, incels may acknowledge their social position without forging an identity as an "incel."

Additionally, some people might identify as incel, even though they are not.

Personal identification as "incel" is neither a necessary nor sufficient quality of inceldom; it really has nothing to do with inceldom.

With that said, others might even fool themselves into believing they are not incels, when they actually are. Consider the statement, "I may be a virgin, but at least I am not incel." This is where the individual deludes himself into thinking that, by distancing himself from "traditional" incels, he will no longer be one later down the road.

Nonetheless, online forums are not seen as a space to push a movement or a superiority system but simply as an outlet where sexually unsuccessful men can gather and post (relatively) freely.

Any adequate, honest, thorough researcher would come to this conclusion.

## 6. "INCELS ARE MOSTLY ALT-RIGHT, WHITE NATIONALISTS."

This, again, is just some strange media invented idea to negatively brand incels. By equating incels with alt-right, Trump supporting white nationalists, the overblown outrage and hate against incels is easier to justify.

The hypocrisy and duplicity of society when it comes to engaging incels serves to exacerbate the animosity. It is also inherently reductive – it lumps all incels under a single socio-political banner, ignoring the reality that incels are in fact troubled individuals with a wide range of problems and *not* a group unified by a set of political beliefs or goals.

An unfortunate dynamic of our current society is that misinformation and reductive commentary comes second nature in most journalism. The pervasiveness of this reality is on display on the media's treatment, and demonization of inceldom.

Once the mainstream started to claim that the majority of incels were white, nationalists it became blatantly obvious that these people simply were not interested in doing the basic work of seeking the truth about incels.

I suppose that media misrepresentations can never really be appreciated until they begin lying about some issue that you are intimately familiar with. It is almost surreal to observe the amount of straight up incel libel being reported as gospel, particularly by the left (and this declaration is coming from someone who leans left himself).

There certainly are a bunch of right-leaning men who would be considered incels, but there are just as many leftists and apolitical incels too.

In incels, we would probably find a similar spread of political affiliations as we would in a sampling of attractive sexually active men. In fact, it would be a safe assumption to claim that sex-having dudes are much more likely to be alt-right leaning Trumpkins than sexless, ugly incels.

After years of observation, I have found that most incels tend to be centrist, or apolitical – which is true of the majority of people in general.

Likewise, the 'white nationalist' label is especially ridiculous.

The members of r/braincels did a poll[18] which generated 1267 responses and found that 54% of the community identified as white, which means that the demographics are similar to the overall racial breakdown in the United States (60.4% non-Hispanic white)[19].

Moreover, a survey conducted on incels.co, which included a sample of 547 responses, noted that the racial demographic breakdown was 56.1% white.[20]

Other research[21] into online incel communities concluded that "there is no definite evidence that Incels.me users are predominantly white, contrary to what is often reported about incels."

Once again, "incel" is not a white supremacy movement or an ideology – it is a state of being.

Even though incels are gathering together online to share experiences, we can rest assured, there is not a massive secret movement of white depressed sexless men out there seeking to overthrow society in a political upheaval.

With that said, we are undergoing a massive drop in overall male productivity, ambition, and economic participation. The male labor force is in decline and has been since the 1960's. This drop has accelerated in recent years.[22]

The future economic consequences of men's nonparticipation in the workforce are still unknown. But this situation has, at least, been recognized by economists and policy makers. What incentive will these men have to advance civilization if society has thrown them into the emerging caste of sexual losers?

Given these existing issues, it is perhaps no surprise that I have observed a sharp rise in collapsitarianism[23] and nihilism — in incel communities. More and more incels are reaching the conclusion that "it's over." They would rather give up and "enjoy the decline," not trying to improve themselves and their situations.

---

## 7. INCELS ARE FUNDAMENTALLY VIOLENT, DANGEROUS TERRORISTS.

---

Authors who make these statements are driven by an agenda, which means they falsify statements, cherrypick negative online forum examples, ignore rational arguments, and deceive readers to make incels look as insane and morally bankrupt as possible.

In other words, the conclusion that incels are "violent, dangerous terrorists" is made before any research even starts.

Take this recent tweet[24] from verified twitter user, Ellen K. Pao, which insinuates that, for some reason, sexless men need to be fired from their occupations. Imagine the outrage if Pao replaced the incel commentary with Muslims or trans people?

One of the explanations that incels are stereotyped as being excessively violent is because of the mischaracterization of the term – "incel."

Labelling any dangerous mass murderer as an "incel" has become trendy clickbait. Some of the most recent mass shooters had girlfriends but were still labelled – "incel" – by media outlets.

Empirical research strongly supports the notion that criminal offenders have more sex partners than non-criminals.[25]

Moreover, gang members also have more sex partners than non-gang members within the same community.[26] Does it make any sense to be presumed dangerous just because one is unable to have sex and is depressed about that fact?

The idea that incels are ticking time-bombs and threats to society is absurd. The primary danger that incels pose is to themselves.

There are an alarming number of incels discussing suicidal ideation, setting dates for when they will kill themselves, and making goodbye posts in their online communities. When will these sad comments be addressed seriously?

---

### 8. "INCELS ARE MOSTLY WOMEN HATING MISOGYNISTS."

---

As mentioned, most incels do not hate women and are not born hateful towards women. For those that do exhibit hatred, it is mostly because they are angry at being born ugly and envious of those men who have more success with the opposite sex.

At this stage, it is not even about a woman, but rather about the man at the individual level. Incels do need to stop the misogyny, but not because it would help them find a girlfriend. It would not.

Incels should stop being misogynists because women are not guilty for their desires. They are not guilty for finding them unattractive. It's not a choice for heterosexual women – it's just their hard-wired biology.

With that noted, while some incels do direct their hatred toward women, the majority direct hatred towards themselves.

There is a deep and alarming enmity directed at their own shortcomings. Incels may sometimes, with twisted logic, blame women for their condition. But usually they consider themselves the true culprits of their own social exclusion and celibacy.

Incels' negative view of women is different than what is commonly understood as misogyny. Incels do not imagine or create a power dynamic between themselves and women, wherein women would be in the inferior position.

A truly misogynistic individual would show contempt towards women for being weak, or dumb, or inferior to men – this hateful person would never seek approval and appreciation – like incels do.

With incels, this whole dynamic is flipped.

Instead of hating women from a position of superiority, incels hate them from a position of inferiority. They believe that women control the levers of the sexual game, and they hate women for excluding them from the game.

While the hatred is the product of a twisted logic, and should in no way be condoned, the fact stands: many incels are, by definition, a group of ineffective men who often feel a paralyzing sense of their own inferiority. So, it is interesting to see people making a big problem out of a group that fundamentally is not a problem.

Not only do the majority of incels hold no views that would be considered dangerous – the ideas they do hold – are ineffective because they are barely noticeable. They only exist in fringe parts of the internet.

Further, there is no core tenet among online incel communities that one must hate women (or any other group) in order to be an incel.

Though this is an unfortunate side-effect, such hatred has never been a primary feature of incel culture and, as far as I know, no online incel forums include misogyny or other assorted bigotry as part of their mission statement or moderation policy.

There are millions of incels all over the world, and although they do ruthlessly mock society because their situations are so messed up, saying that every single one of them is a radical, violent, woman-hating terrorist waiting to destroy the world is every bit as unfair as saying that every single Muslim is a potential suicide bomber.

# II. WHAT IS THE BLACKPILL?

Life is a game of inches.

We have probably heard a similar phrase before — it is typically used in the context of sports. In the context of this book, it represents a fundamental truth; it pertains to every facet of your social and psychological life.

The inches — and the centimeters, and the millimeters — matter.

Your height, your frame, your jawline, your forehead, your nose, your eyes, your lips, your genitals and more represent this truth.

It cannot be overstated how much the size, shape, and length of these features affect not only your romantic and sexual prospects, but almost every aspect of your life.

The blackpill essentially states that our dating choices are based off of pure biological determinism. And if you do not meet an attractiveness threshold, the chances of having a happy, fulfilled relationship will be near impossible.

"Taking the blackpill" basically means developing an awareness of a true biological reality that can be disempowering. Often, it means submitting to the fact of one's own biological unfitness. To the fact that one will never achieve the sexual or romantic life that one hopes for. That one may never even have sex.

Yes, from birth, the deck can be so stacked against some people – that it can never be beaten.

In its simplest form the theory states that our genetics determine the quality of our life and the quality of our relationships. With a blackpill awareness we know that everything we have been told about romance, love, and sex is wrong – it does not really just "happen."

It's not about effort, and it's not about the changes and adjustments you make to yourself, your appearance, or your behavior. Nothing you do will change it.

Remember back in high school when the most popular boys were also the best looking? Not a coincidence. And that is what can be so demoralizing about the blackpill.

It really does not matter how nice of a personality one has, or what music he listens to, or what brand of clothing he wears. Those who say that such things matter are simply lying to seem morally virtuous.

For those who have already swallowed the blackpill, it is not a secret that "looks" are far more important than "personality." Only those ignorant or in denial in regards to blackpill science argue otherwise. Biological determinism is a scary concept. It implies that no matter what you do you will never be better than what you were intended to be.

## THE REFUTATION OF THE "JUST-WORLD" FALLACY

So why do so many people deny the reality of the blackpill? Most of it has to do with the just world fallacy.

As humans, we like to believe we are in control of the outcomes of our lives, for better or for worse. We also believe that most of our success is the result of something that we did. Success, we believe, is earned through our intentional effort.

Sometimes we might even feel morally superior to others when we compare our own successes to others' lack of success. We may deduce, from this imbalance, that other people are lazy or irresponsible. We may believe "being poor" is indicative of people's character rather than it being a systematic oppression.

The "just-world" fallacy is at the root of all this. The idea that everything can be earned through human effort and control can drive some nasty, inhumane beliefs.

We do not like to recognize harder truths. For instance, to extend the above example, that in order for rich people to thrive, others must barely survive.

You commonly see these attitudes among members of the Baby Boomer generation. These people want everyone to believe that they acquired their wealth through 100% hard work. In reality, Boomer's success was ~90% luck of being born at the right time and ~10% their own hard work.

And what about all the people, of the very same generation, who fell through the cracks? What about the people of color excluded by systemic racism, or gay people forced to keep their sexuality hidden or face violence and social persecution?

Boomers latched onto an image of mainstream success that conveniently ignored these vast problems. In the 1970s and up to the mid 1980s, one could work a blue-collar job on a single salary and then buy a decent property. Impossible today.

Nowadays even the mainstream view of things is much direr, to say nothing of the real situation on the ground. Younger people have to deal with:

automation, foolishly high costs of university education (often to obtain worthless degrees), massive debt, criminally high property costs, globalization, underemployment, and economic instability.

In the 1970s, if an employer had a high-ranking job to offer, advertisements were placed in the local newspapers — resulting in maybe three or four qualified candidates applying for the open position.

Today, employers simply post job advertisements online, which result in thousands of qualified candidates applying from across the country, despite ridiculously high expectations placed on them by the employer.

The "just work hard" belief system is just a farcical lie pushed upon us at an early age to keep us motivated. It has no bearing in present reality — it is almost comical to believe in it in 2019.

And yet the "just-world" fallacy and the belief in hard work die hard. They make everything in life seem fair and as though the future is completely under our control.

As we grind away at that tiresome 9-5 job, which we absolutely cannot stand, while witnessing professional athletes such as LeBron James playing a game for millions of dollars, we rationalize in our mind that he is at the professional level due to "hard work" – so hypothetically, we could have accomplished similarly, if only we would have taken up an invested interest in basketball and "worked hard" such as he did.

But that is not true. The truth is: LeBron James has elite-tier genetics. Hard work, knowledge, and focus contribute to his mastery of the game, but these would be pointless without his stature.

He is tremendously tall, wide-framed, long-armed, and has a natural muscularity – that would have taken years of training for most to achieve. He did not "earn" his genes – he got lucky.

Yes, with enough "hard work" we all could have gotten better at playing basketball, but we would never have been the world-class 6'8" NBA superstar that is known across the globe as "King James."

We avoid acknowledging the genetics part of success because it makes things seem very unfair. It crushes our treasured sense of life's essential justice.

There are absolutely people out there who grinded just as hard as LeBron did at basketball but today work regular-ass, boring occupations because they did not possess the innate traits to craft themselves into professional athletes.

This book will explain why our genes and early developmental influences demarcate our potential for success, basically setting the cap on what one can achieve.

If the genetic preconditions are present, success is then a linear trajectory, and hard work refines it and keeps it moving forward. If the genetic preconditions are absent, any amount of work is just a futile expenditure of effort. If someone is repeatedly struggling at something, he or she is simply operating outside the controls of their inherent competencies.

No man with an IQ of 75 is going to become an astrophysicist, no matter how hard he tries.

A lot of extremely successful people tend to ignore both the role of genes and of just pure luck when discussing their accomplishments. Recently, this trend was even documented scientifically as physically attractive individuals are stronger endorsers of the belief in a just world.[1]

Beyond the science, take Dwayne "The Rock" Johnson as a case study. He's a childhood idol for many young boys – he was even one of mine.

The Rock's dad was a professional wrestler. As such, he was born into a wrestling foothold and was able to get into an extremely tough industry through nepotism. From his eventual wrestling successes, he was then able to transition into one of the most famously narcissistic industries in the world: Hollywood.

Despite this career move, The Rock loves to showcase his humility by telling the story about he came from nothing, with only $7 to his name, before ascending to superstar status.

Take the following quote from The Rock as an example:

"What's the key to success? The key is, there is no key. Be humble, hungry, and the hardest worker in any room."

Here The Rock congratulates himself for always being the hardest, hungriest worker in the room and this hard-work is what he credits to his achievements. The paradox here is that this is a complete middle finger to those who also worked their asses off but never landed that big break.

Since The Rock was struggling with poverty and depression, what did he do about it? He became a 6'4" wide framed, handsome, professional wrestler, and actor.

It's just that easy, bro.

Let's be frank, The Rock was born into an incredibly lucky situation and this luck propelled him to movie star status.

If he were born as a 5'7" small framed, average-looking guy whose father who worked at Home Depot, he would not be where he is today.

This isn't even touching the fact that The Rock's dad was an actual professional wrestler, who could train him and provide insider access into the sport.

The Rock also, again, enjoyed the genetic gifts of being 6'4" tall, with a handsome face, a wide frame, and a deep, sexy voice. He was naturally a nearly ideal physical specimen to be groomed and built up and marketed to professional wrestling audiences.

In defense of Dwayne, many famous people who have won the genetic lottery make this fundamental attribution error[2] — stressing to the masses that "hard-work" was the crucial factor on the road to their personal success.

And they subconsciously brainwash themselves that they had complete control over the stellar outcomes of their lives. In reality, most are either born and bred as a success, or not.

So, the next time The Rock parades his, "just work hard, bro!" speech, please know that he is entirely full of shit.

It would be akin to reading a book from a Victoria's Secret "angel" teaching a teenage girl how to become a successful international model (whose body shapes are impossible for 95% of women to ever achieve).

In terms of dating, in a "just-world" men would be judged by their character, not by immutable traits such as skin color, the angle of their jawline, or the length of their limbs.

This is why normies tell men that if you "just be nice" and "have interesting hobbies" and "be funny," you can have a romantic relationship with a girl, too! When it comes to giving incels dating advice, normies typically offer what amounts to these worthless platitudes such as taking a shower, finding a cool hobby, being a nice guy, or to stop existing as a misogynist.

And they are 100% serious with these suggestions; they are seeing the world through the filter of the "just-world" fallacy.

Admittedly, this advice *can't* hurt and it *might* help, so why shouldn't incels try these straightforward normie suggestions?

It is insufficient.

Ideologically, self-improvement as a concept is simply a way that social expectations oppress incels, giving them a false hope that if they do abide by society's rules and uphold society's norms of civility, and hygiene, and kindness, then they will be rewarded.

But this is, for the most part, a delusion. These basic recommendations will not improve their lives in any meaningful way and it certainly will not do so immediately or reliably.

# III. THE BACKGROUND OF THE BLACKPILL

This section explores the idea that there is, in some way, a standard nature of women. It will not be comparison between the sexual desires of women versus those of men. The emphasis will be predominantly on the mating strategies of women and how this relates to incelibate men.

Evolutive reality is by definition sexist. Men provide; women have babies.

Evolution has encoded into women that they be attracted to both heritable traits (i.e. genes) and providers (i.e. resources) so that they can produce viable offspring. In the modern climate, this reality – for some reason – has become hard for many to accept. The idea that humans have evolved beyond our innate proclivities sounds nice but these traits are still fundamental parts of who we really are, for right or wrong.

With that said, it is women who tend to pursue long-term relationships, pragmatically. They select lifelong mates founded on a companionate love based on both genetic markers and/or access to resources.

Men are hardwired to select younger partners who look like they are good for breeding – ignoring ambition, career, financial security, and intelligence. This is why the petite blonde 23-year-old Starbucks barista making only minimum wage can be more appealing to a man in comparison to the 45-year-old career women making over six figures a year as an attorney.

To place this tendency into perspective, observe the figure[1] on the next page: men of all ages prefer women in their early 20s.

It bears reciting again, men are the irrational selectors in the mating market. Women are the rational ones. And there is nothing terribly wrong with that, as long as we do not pretend reality is something that it is not, which we have been doing as a society for the last century or so.

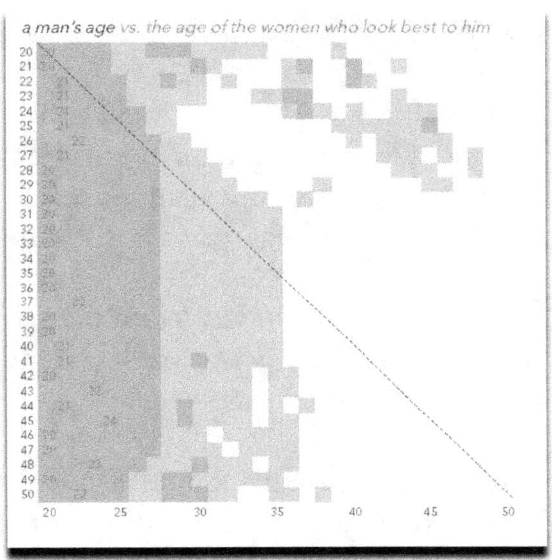


When the behaviors and mating preferences of women are discussed, we are talking about observable events that they precipitate.

If I say human sexuality is immoral most would agree; if I say men's sexuality is immoral, most would agree with that as well; and if I say women's sexuality is immoral it should be met with the same response. But it is not. So, before anyone suggests that this book is "hating" on women for pointing out these realities, that would be incorrect.

Do not conflate the truth with hate, it is important to recognize the difference between the two.

It needs mentioning that women do think individually and all women are different. Each has her own unique set of hopes and dreams and thoughts – just as every fingerprint is also unique.

But all of us have descended from only those women who sought the best genes – a tendency still highly demonstrated today.

Therefore, even though all women are different, they still evolved under the inclinations of being subconsciously attracted to men of high reproductive potential. This is called sexual selection, most of us probably learned about it in our 6th grade science classes.

We can observe this in nearly all species – preferences for certain traits. In our modern world, this preference does not even need to be related to some type of genetic advantage.

A blue-eyed, symmetrically beautiful faced stud, with a full head of hair is useless in the savanna. He serves no practical use, he is just pretty.

So, women might be attracted to facial harmony or a prominent jawbone or a deep voice or blue eyes in a partner. But these traits do not necessarily give men any relevant genetic advantage of survival, in fact they can often be detrimental.

As a simple example, taller men do not live as long as shorter men. In a more elaborate illustration, genetic fitness (advantage) is relative to an environmental context and can change over time – shorter men, for instance, can be genetically superior during times of famine or in circumstances with a limited food supply (e.g. isolated islands) since height and weight correlates with basal metabolic rate.

It is hard to deny that our evolution has been sexual. Of course, we also inherited traits to survive and to eat and to learn. But above all these is the tendency to reproduce.

Humans are mammals. In all mammal species, females have far more value than males. Women are competitively sought after and they are more coveted.

This is largely because each woman has only a few eggs and pregnancy removes her from the reproductive market for nearly a year. This makes fertile, available women rarer.

Contrastingly, men can yield sperm on a continuous basis, so they can reproduce with an unlimited number of partners.

The comparative scarcity of fertile women gives them higher value than fertile men. For this reason, women are very picky about their choice of a mate; selecting for quality is an optimal reproductive strategy.

If the strategy is to maximize reproduction, women should only expel energy raising genetically exceptional children, while males should not be selective, but should attempt to reproduce with as many women as possible with the intention of having as many children as possible.

As long as we are not discussing humans, this is the oldest accepted truth in biology. If we say this about chimpanzees, everyone agrees — it is an observable truth. But if we say it about humans, our biases take over.

The assertion has too many personal consequences.

Only the dedicated thinkers ask the question, "why is the idea that biology dictates considerable factors among sexes verboten?"

As much as it seems some want to believe, biology cannot be unlearned. Watch any nature program, and you will see male animals fighting to the death for the chance to secure a mating opportunity from the female.

This same scenario applies to humans to a lesser degree because we have retained most of these evolutive brain mechanisms.

The chimpanzee, which is exceptionally close to us genetically, forms a society riddled with violence where access to younger female is only secured by the healthiest and strongest male.

In humans, it is not necessarily violence or strength but looks which are the primary factor in deciding whether or not a potential mate is attractive. This has been proven over and over again by several studies.

Interestingly, the common belief that the way you look is a proxy for vitality and health, is not necessarily true. Indicators of attractiveness (facial symmetry, a man's deep voice, chiseled chin, women's hourglass figure, etc.) are generally unrelated to health and ability.[2]

Our strong preference for these features has likely evolved in a positive feedback loop,[3] and not because they signal health or ability.

Despite the reproductive uselessness of symmetric face and a positive canthal tilt our primitive brains are still wired to find those traits attractive. This is called the attractiveness halo effect[4]; it is pervasive in our social interactions, starting in the teenage years.

This is also why, when we hear the expression, "confidence is sexy," it should be recognized for what it really is — sexiness. Sexiness is sexy — confident because attractive, not the other way around. Confidence is a self-feeding cycle.

It just so happens that sexy, attractive people are confident.

The halo effect is everywhere, especially when it comes to female-male sexual relations. We convince ourselves that an individual possesses numerous other positive qualities when we find them attractive, otherwise we would need to openly admit that we are naturally shallow.

The perception we have of the beautiful seems to be born out of confirmation bias – attributing a positive quality and aura to individuals that we are predisposed to view positively due to other, more *tangible* reasons, which also causes others to admire them, which in turn lends the attractive person to be "confident".

Plenty of people are confident or self-assured and still socially rejected – in fact, the more confident an ugly person is, the more severe the social rejection.

A funny observation is to recognize that most academics have zero issue slamming the attempts by creationists to get intelligent design and even biblical creationism into schools.

And rightfully so. Almost to a person they all accept evolution by natural selection as the proper explanation of the diversity of the species.

That noted, many of these same academics also seem to believe gender to be a complete social construct. The hard biological and psychological research on the subject is conveniently ignored.

But a true belief in evolution requires the acknowledgement that pressures exist that influence *everything* about us, especially dating.

One of the greatest tragedies of humans is our hubris. We delude ourselves into thinking we are better than animals, that we have ascended so far beyond them. This just is not true: we are animals. Our hind brain influences our decisions whether we like to think so or not; we still run on similar operating systems as other mammals. And for some, this influence is stronger than others.

The author of *The Righteous Mind* (Jonathan Haidt) characterizes the human mind using the metaphor of the elephant and the rider. For Haidt, the human mind is a partnership between separate but connected entities.

We like to believe we are the rider (all that is conscious), and as the rider we can steer the elephant (all that is automatic) to travel in a certain direction. However, when it comes down to it, the elephant controls the show.

Human nature is also a product of culture, just as culture is a product of human nature. So, it is important to recognize that women's preferences are not "all based on genes." There are also social explanations.

Sexual selection is always relative – individuals are selected by comparison against other individuals, not against some idealized figure that may or may not exist.

This is because there is no evidence that the mechanism of sexual selection can by itself come to disqualify almost all members of a gender, so there is zero reason to assume that this is particularly the situation with humans right now.

As such, the explanation that cultural factors, rather than pure biology, are responsible for women's current dating standards, is just as viable. There is plenty of evidence of cultural factors affecting what is considered as attractive. I elaborate more on these cultural dynamics in Chapter V.

To summarize, women and men have different standards because we are different. Biologically, men compete to have sex with as many girls as possible, and women compete to have sex with the single best man (or men) as possible, **and** then getting him to provide for her (see: Dual Mating Strategy & Hypergamy section). The roles are basically inverses of each other because our biology is inverse to each other.

A man is envied if he sleeps with many women and a woman is envied if she gains the commitment from a great guy.

There are strengths and weaknesses to both sexes. The female duality works out fine, so long as we accept that male competition is part of our existence. This is a product of nature, of evolution.

This goes to shit when technology advances quicker than the time it takes for evolution to adapt properly, causing strange centralized social norms and a society that does not even acknowledge the duality.

This is partly why everyone today is so confused and depressed and anxious. Which results in *losers* like me, who decide to spend too much time, writing books such as this one, attempting to figure it all out.

Anyways, how did we, as a society, reach this blackpilled stage? The following sections provide a brief history.

---

## THE BLUEPILL

---

Most of us were raised under the influence of the so-called bluepill. A bluepiller believes in the mantra that if a heterosexual man works hard and is a nice guy, he will be rewarded with a caring, loyal, loving girlfriend. In other words, a nice guy's dedication to a career or a craft will pay off eventually, in the form of a valued relationship.

Be nice --> Be productive --> Get a girlfriend.

This framework is so designed as to draw on inherent male instincts, such as being protective towards women and to view females as the purer sex. These beliefs were instilled into men so they could someday provide for a family.

Through the bluepill lens, assuming a heteronormative and patriarchally organized nuclear family unit, the man fulfilled the role of working outside the home to provide the money required to support the family. While the woman plays the role as the caregiver for the family; being responsible for the primary socialization of the children while providing cohesion for the group through emotional support and social instruction.

These are simple but effective ideological constraints, at least in terms of societal progress, especially during a time before women could provide for themselves, as they can today.

Regardless of whether or not we want to believe in the stereotypical ideas about gender roles, these expectations were useful for a functional society. Men were encouraged to be more chivalrous and respectful, as these were valued characteristics in a man at the time. In return for his chivalry, that man would seek a woman who was classy, polite, innocent and respectful.

Members of both sexes would be flexing their potential as good long-term partners by adhering to these expectations. Each sex displayed a propensity to be great mothers and fathers and heads of a family unit; it was a transaction, traditional father for traditional mother. One could argue that the bluepill was a state of blissful ignorance.

Interestingly, the traditional fantasy of the bluepill lifestyle, in terms of individual relationships, is fascinatingly misogynistic. Why should a man be rewarded with a woman simply because he is a "nice chivalrous guy" with "a good career"?

In this sense, the bluepill perspective is a construct wherein certain attributes are projected onto women by men in order to elicit their voluntary sacrifice.

The idea that any nice man with a decent job is deserving of a partner has a moral dimension. If he does these simple things, he is seen as an upstanding and morally acceptable person. As such, the bluepilled man determines that women should now be interested in him simply because of his kindness and economic stability.

Nevertheless, as a result of the bluepill illusion, the man begins to hate himself and feel defective. Because after following all the bluepill advice of improving his personality he *still* finds himself without any romantic success. And after several unsuccessful dating attempts, he then comes to the conclusion that he is an unwanted, unworthy person.

Why would he reach this conclusion? Because bluepill societal conditioning suggests that the number one criterion women use to select a partner is character. So, if the man cannot successfully find a woman to date, what other conclusion can he, as a bluepiller, reach other than that his character is irreparably flawed?

Of course, women are not under any moral obligation to consider men dating material just simply because they are nice and employable. She has zero responsibility to date any man who believed that since he was "playing by the rules" that he would ultimately be rewarded with a partner.

The bluepilled man, as a result, will undoubtedly develop resentment and also, begin looking for solutions to his shattered worldview. The bluepill was supposed to represent comfort and security, but it has only brought him disappointment and pain.

---

## THE REDPILL

---

The term redpill originates from the movie, "The Matrix." The premise behind that movie is that everything we see is an illusion, that we are living inside a matrix, a huge computer which generates what we perceive to be reality. But that actual reality is different from what the one we are observing.

Becoming "redpilled" is often used to refer to a process by which a person's perspective is dramatically transformed, introducing them to a new understanding of the true nature of a particular situation.

The redpill rose to popularity around the late 1990s, largely coinciding with the rise of the internet. During the time, men started to gather together digitally to their share thoughts and experiences with dating, relationships, and marriage.

For the men of the time period who struggled to find dates, the redpill perspective was a valuable resource. It also allowed the men who were *successful* in the dating game to discuss both relationship dynamics and mating problems.

For instance, many men were led to the redpill because they were in search of answers for their divorce or their partner's infidelity. With the shared thoughts among various men, patterns started to emerge, offering numerous explanations for mating conditions, which redpilled men used to develop theories attempting to explain women.

Also around this time, the Pickup Artist (PUA)[5] movement became popular; it was pioneered by bloggers like Mystery and Heartiste, who expanded upon what routines and strategies men could use to attract women.

More and more collective wisdom was shared over blogs and internet forums and from these different cyber camps, the manosphere, soon materialized.

With this knowledge, the redpiller uncovered how formulaic human relationships were and as such, exploited that information towards finding a partner for sex and/or a relationship.

In the simplest terms, the redpill is about amassing information and gathering observations about women, with a concentration on relationships and sex. In terms of dating and sex, the theoretical framework of the redpill was the common response to the bluepill illusion most men were brought up believing (work hard and be rewarded with sex and/or a girlfriend).

With the lessons of the collected redpill material, men could now gain a greater understanding of human behavior, then exploit this understanding to improve himself and make better dating decisions.

The red pills optimistic objective is to "fix" men so that they can be successful with life and relationships. Many would describe it as self-empowering, although the goal is not always about love or money, but also casual sex.

The focus of the redpill, as is commonly claimed, is on the present and the future. How a man is now, but ensuring he will be a better person later in the life.

The philosophy stresses being reliant on yourself for happiness instead of being reliant on validation from the opposite sex. The redpill is indeed a sexual strategy and it does work for some. It is an approach for guys who have normal to above normal looks, but aren't naturally super-attractive, or are otherwise socially hapless.

Think of a guy who would be almost be traditionally handsome but is not quite there; maybe he was raised under bluepill ideology and just needed to be more assertive or confident. Something easily fixable. In other words, guys who are at least average-looking, but still cannot get laid due to having high inhibition or some other personality quirk.

But the redpill doesn't acknowledge that some people are just completely screwed, and no amount of game and behavior will really help. It takes a different perspective to recognize this sad fact.

With this in mind, we fast forward to today and the birth of the blackpill theory, which is mostly only discussed by incels. According to the blackpill, no amount of self-improvement will help if the man does not meet a certain threshold in basic attractiveness; these are the immutable genetics in which you are born with and cannot change.

Once again, the blackpill accepts that men and women have different mindsets of desirability and sexual selection. The blackpill also recognizes that modern society has undergone certain cultural shifts, mainly beginning in the 1960's, that have made sexual promiscuity acceptable.

Some of the contributing factors for this social change include: the availability of birth control, the decline of religion as a mainstream moral force, changes in media portrayal of sex, social media, and dating apps.

The civilized mating patterns of the past (monogamous partnering and nuclear families) are being replaced by whatever confusing type of mating market we have today?

Most people are under the impression that sexual liberation would grant sexual access to more people, but this is not true. The truth is that with promiscuity, a large percentage of men are excluded.

When women are not being pressured into marriage and can provide for themselves, they will pursue mating partners on an equal or higher playing field – this has been largely observed in sociological dating study after sociological dating study.

To conclude this section, consider the three pills: blue, red, and black.

They all represent different time periods and responses to the sexual market, but the blackpill is inherently the least misogynistic.

The bluepiller is arguably all about being a nice, stable guy who places women on a pedestal, in the hopes that his kindness and provision will be attuned with romance.

The redpiller is arguably all about being charming and manipulative, while exercising a refined attitude, that has been honed for months, to trigger certain psychological inputs in a woman, in the hope that his "game" will be attuned with romance.

While the blackpiller simply acknowledges that women are physically attracted to whomever they are physically attracted to.

Surprisingly, the blackpill correctly identifies the female sexual revolution. It is ironic, then, that the people who subscribe to the blackpill point of view are the ones most often being labelled as the most misogynist.

# IV. LIFE IS EASIER WHEN YOU ARE ATTRACTIVE

Digging into the plethora of rigorously, peer-reviewed social scientific research from field-leading Ph.D.'s, at respected academic institutions suggests that attractive people, of both sexes, are perceived differently. Duh.

We will begin with one of the more deflating examples to showcase the attractiveness advantage – the "beauty premium." This term refers to the positive correlation between physical desirability and earnings.

In a pivotal study, researchers noted that the scope of the beauty premium is analogous to both the racial and gender games in economical attainment in the United States labor market.[1] They found that above average-looking workers earned about 10-15% more than workers who had below-average looks.

Other research[2] in this emerging field, notes that physically attractive workers have higher confidence, which in turn, leads to increased wages.

Moreover, physically attractive individuals are perceived as more sociable, dominant, sexually capable, intelligent, and mentally healthy. They also tend to have better all-around social skills than physically unattractive people.[3]

Funny people are considered sexy too, but not for reasons that you think. When a funny person comes off as sexy, it's their sexiness that makes them funny and not the other way around.[4]

Unsurprisingly, it is safe to conclude that attractive people just have better overall life experiences.[5]

It is certainly no secret that strangers are more kind to you if you are good-looking. They are more likely to smile when you walk by. People are more likely to gravitate toward you and pursue friendships with you. Potential partners are more receptive to advances. The list goes on and on.

Good-looking people are even less likely to be convicted for a crime and get lower sentences on average, all as a result of being physically attractive.[6]

On the other end of the spectrum physical unattractiveness is positively correlated with lower socioeconomic status, lower educational attainment, lower IQ, poorer health, not owning a home, being unemployed and also not being married.[7] Damn.

Just like those individuals who "sound black" over the phone or those who have a name like LaKeisha will have a harder time getting a job than basic white-ass Johnathan[8], being disadvantaged in attractiveness can and does make life more challenging. The same type of bias permeates all of society.

In sum, life and relationship success is still possible for the ugly, but it is a lot harder. Sadly, this attractiveness standard is present even in the eyes of a newborn infant, suggesting it is simply an innate human preference, rather than learned.[9]

It is also no secret that naturally good-looking men receive a lot of positive attention from women.

This could be through flirting, admiration, sex, intimacy, or a relationship.

Women are more likely to sleep with you, without a condom, too – as the more attractive a man was judged to be, the less likely women (ages 18-32) were to intend to use protection during sex.[10]

Women also benefit intimately from having sex with hot dudes. The number one factor determining whether women orgasm during sex or not, is their partners' physical attractiveness.[11] Suggesting quality sex is not about sexual "technique" or "skill" but just about being *hott*.

I guess it is no surprise then that research suggests that multiple orgasms are more likely when women are partnered with an attractive man.[12]

With the above discoveries acknowledged, the existence of naturally attractive man does not mean that all women can get into a committed relationship with the archetype, nor that some women will not be limited by certain things such distance or religious values, and it does not mean that an 'Average Joe' cannot get into a relationship the traditional way.

The Pareto principal[13] implies that 80% of men just have a lower success rate with women than men in the top 20% of "sexiness" do. The principle suggests that these 20% of men are responsible for 80% of the sex with women. Accordingly, under the blackpill, many men are incapable of ever achieving that "sexy" level (being in the top 20% of men).

We even have Tinder data from 2019[14] suggesting that women only *like* (swipe-right on) 4.5% of men. Considering this, it can be argued that we should revise the original 80/20 distribution to a 95/5 distribution when it comes to modern-day dating.

Numbers aside, good-looking men have more romantic options. There's nothing earth shattering about this assertion.

Just like the top 1% of the richest people owning 90% of the wealth does not mean that everyone else must be starving, the '80/20 rule' simply states that 20% of men, the most attractive men, have the greatest market-share of sexual partners.

Incels, who are at the bottom of this distribution hierarchy, are the ones who cannot get into any relationship whatsoever, and only slightly above them are those who are unable to attract a woman except with their financial resources, usually at a much older age, when they are financially secure.[15]

This is all fairly well documented scientifically.

Even if we do not want to believe in the 20% number or the 4.5% number we cannot deny that dating apps and websites allow attractive men to cast wider nets and monopolize larger portions of the mating market than they were able to before the popularization of such technology. It is just an observable reality that men now have to compete with other men across an entire city, not just at a bar or in a particular social circle.

This is not a "rule," but an overwhelming, implicit trend in our society. Making these trends explicit leads to push back because everyone likes to think their destiny is in their own hands. (There's that "just-world" fallacy again).

In reality, we all have a target we are trying to hit. Some men have a rifle, trying to hit the broadside of a barn 10 feet away in an open field. Others are trying to throw a rock at a nickel two miles away on the other side of a rainforest.

This has nothing to do with personal virtue and everything to do with luck.

The deck absolutely is stacked. But the people for whom it is stacked in their favor do not like admitting this, because it takes away from them and can cause them emotional pain. They would much rather believe that they are earning their success, sexual or otherwise, than admit that it's fallen into their laps.

## THE IMPORTANCE OF SEX

When it comes to proving their point, critics will attempt to push an agenda, almost ubiquitously, by claiming that sex is not as important as incels believe it to be. The value of sex for men is completely diminished in this criticism, which absurdly tries to suggest that sex is not required for a fulfilled life. This is nonsense.

Once you realize that intimate, human contact is one of our basic core needs, analogous to basic needs like eating nutritious foods or accessing shelter, then the criticism loses all credibility.

Lack of sex and intimacy has been linked to feelings of self-loathing, low self-esteem, outward-facing rage and possibly even violence. This type of negative feedback can start a vicious cycle, that is difficult to escape from.

An incel cannot just turn off his desire for intimacy and turn asexual.

Incels are upset by their predicament because it is just a basic human response to be frustrated and saddened about feeling by a lack of access to a basic human need. Especially as they watch others acquiring this need in abundance, with minimal effort.

Across multiple studies[16], sex is directly linked to happiness and health. So, without intercourse, an incel is warranted if he experiences emotions such as bitterness and depression. And of course, like all humans, incels have strong needs in both physical and emotional areas.

Additional research found a positive association between the frequency and importance of sexual behavior (holding hands, hugging, kissing, mutual stroking, masturbating, and intercourse) and quality of life.[17]

Sex is also linked to lower mortality in young men.[18] Clearly, the oxytocin released during intimate physical activity with another warm person is important to mental and physical well-being.

Incels have commented that even the tiniest glimpses of affection from women have made them feel better for an entire day. The mere brushing of arms with another person can elicit an immense positive response. These bodily senses actually create, and have an effect on, feelings and emotions.

So, it is not just the intercourse which is absent in these men's lives. Incels are also lacking full spectrum of sight, sound, taste, smell, and touch of another person.

At its root, that is what sex really is all about, all of the different senses working in unison, bringing a pleasurable sensation and experiences long enough for a chance of reproduction. It is arguably our greatest human high – enjoying intimacy together.

It's no wonder that at the very basic level Maslow's Hierarchy of Needs[19] right next to food and shelter, is reproduction. According to this popular motivational theory, each triangle must be traversed linearly (i.e., from top to bottom) before self-actualization can be achieved.

Although it does have some heavy criticisms[20], Maslow's Hierarchy is still one of our main holistic theories of motivation, and incels are missing three of its core elements.

# MENTAL HEALTH & SOCIAL EXCLUSION

An important aspect of positive mental health is to feel good about something, to feel both valuable and valued. We get this positive reinforcement from a variety of sources, including our family, peers, work, and social media.

Beyond that our value comes from our personal achievements: money, fame, educational attainment, and other accomplishments. Relationships and even *love* both fall under achievements. These all give us confidence and increase our self-esteem.

Genetics can also fulfill one with similar conviction. As a man your height, facial structure, musculature, and intelligence can give you a sense of value. A tall, handsome, athletic, and intelligent man will be fulfilled with "value" throughout his entire life.

A guy on the opposite end of the spectrum, can still achieve value but it will be unbelievably challenging. That is why the blackpill can be so dark for a young man who isn't born attractive or gifted.

Never forget that the 6'3", square jawed man who won the genetic lottery by chance could also tomorrow be hit by a car and be left paralyzed from the neck down, even if this individual generally is a good person.

This why it is so easy for us to hate the blackpill. We want to believe that if we do the right things we will be safe and sound. That hard work will bring success. That being kind will be reciprocated. All these beliefs come crashing down if we admit that our success and happiness depends heavily on pure dumb luck.

Like anyone else, incels do want to be happy. But nearly all of them share in common, that no matter hard that they tried, they are incapable of changing their dire situation.

This cannot be emphasized enough — a lack of affection is not some isolated compartment of the human psyche that we can just convince incels to close or ignore when things are not going well.

Failing to build or create intimacy, especially during a time when all your peers are successfully doing so, can impact just about every aspect of your life. This starts at a very early age, as secondary sex characteristics (body hair, muscle mass, height) can have a massive effect on the lives of many young men. The difference in the tempo of development of these characteristics has key psychological and social consequences.[21]

More advanced adolescents are likely to dominate less advanced classmates in stereotypical hegemoically masculine values. In western culture, valued traits include competitiveness and independence, but also physical characteristics such as muscularity, athletic prowess, and eliciting romantic interest from the opposite sex.

As a result, pubescent boys begin to measure themselves against their most physically advanced peers, especially those who become stronger and taller. By comparing themselves to these genetically lucky peers, late developers might begin to question their masculine performance and their physical presence. Particularly, masculine self-esteem issues often start here.

Boys who do not develop preferred traits right away start to wonder how tall they will become, when their muscles will grow, if and when they will experience their first kiss. As others start attaining these things, those who do not can develop these marginalized feelings. The feelings, in turn, can provoke considerable behavioral repercussions.

Ideally, youth is a series of feedback loops which establish confidence in oneself. A young individual is supposed to grow and mature by facing youth's particular challenges – puberty, embarrassment, social difficulties, growing sexual identity – and learning that they are survivable, and integrating them into their personality.

As incels fail to experience life's challenges as a form of confidence-building, their serious problems begin.

The downward spiral begins for many incels approximately in their early teenage years.

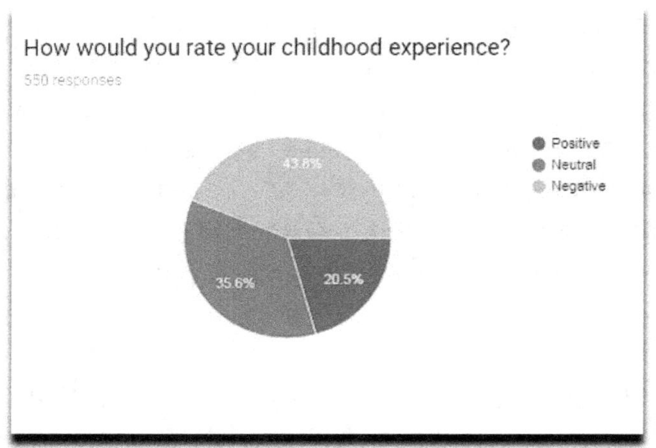


From a survey on incels.co, currently the largest incel forum in the incelosphere, only 20.5% of incels rated their childhood experience as positive. 43.8% of them had negative childhood experiences, while 35.6% rated their childhood as neutral.[22]

During adolescence, hierarchies surface which split teenagers into distinct classes by virtue of their value. Value, at this age, is largely determined by beauty, where the popular students are often the best-looking.

A difficult period for any adolescent, but particularly for an unattractive man. Male peers begin to look down upon other males who are not successful with the opposite sex. As a result, romantically unsuccessful teens began to suffer socially. The interplay of energy and enthusiasm lower – the base vitality which is often essential to feel positive about oneself.

The emotional and mental anguish does not immediately start out as a tragedy but as it continues, it will slowly grind a person down and seep into every other part of his existence.

When one cannot acquire romantic interest, it will breed feelings of insecurity, inadequacy and depression. Depression, especially, can poison everything as it will sap your energy and make the overall condition worse. But insecurity is a destroyer in its own right, especially because it is also a very unattractive trait.

Although incels lack access to physical needs or romantic prospects with women, many still wish to satisfy emotional needs through family relationships or male friendships. Unfortunately, as expressed, inceldom status presents itself as low status to everyone — the insecurity and lack of confidence present in most incels makes them unattractive as friends and confidants. It rubs all people — not just prospective romantic partners — the wrong way.

One of the sadder themes apparent in my research was the prevalence of extreme loneliness amongst incels. Which is not all that particularly surprising considering loneliness is an emerging public health issue, not just in inceldom, but across the general population.

A survey conducted by Cigna[23] suggested that social media based communities are boosting levels of loneliness in the United States, thereby undermining the nation's collective mental and physical health. The research noted widespread loneliness, with nearly half of Americans reporting they feel alone, isolated, or left out at least some of the time. This issue is mostly affecting younger adults: 75 million millennials (ages 23-37) and generation Z-ers (18-22) report loneliness more than does any other United States demographic.

For the incel who has trouble forming bonds with others, this is a predictable trend. This is partly because inceldom omits lower status to other men which has a systemic like effect to all other phases of life.

As such, the inescapable nature of being considered ugly is devastating, because one will likely not be treated as respectfully as others. This mistreatment has massive psychological effects which compound upon one another. The original problem – unattractiveness – can start to blanket one's entire life. It becomes the bedrock of all social interaction.

Little extant literature exists on the relationship between emotional and physiological development, but the information that does exist supports the idea that emotional attitudes are connected to physiological events. And the emotional traumas specific to unattractive teenaged boys will carry over into social difficulties in adulthood. They often become inescapable. The feelings of loneliness are engrained within – they are definitive aspects of the young man's personality now, and cannot be easily shaken off.

The number of people who can remain happy without any relationships, not to mention friends, is *very* small. In fact, there is a wealth of scientific research that prolonged loneliness will progressively erode your cognition[24], destroy your physical health in almost every way imaginable[25], and increase the chances of suicide.[26]

Instead of recognizing the core issues at work, our culture instead proposes, with condescension, that an incel simply improve upon his 5'4" height and disfigured face by spending months at the gym, getting a new haircut, taking a shower, and buying fancy new clothing.

It is suggested that he join clubs, work harder to excel in his career, and become the center of his social circle. We encourage him to radiate happiness, to be charismatic, and to be funny. And to do all of that while being alone and depressed.

To do *all* of that while shouldering the weight of extreme self-loathing. Then maybe, just maybe, if he overcomes all odds, he will get a *chance* at human affection.

Brutal.

# V. WHAT WOMEN FIND ATTRACTIVE

The information presented in this chapter is predominantly based upon scientific literature which has been peer-reviewed. It is not intended to push any specific agenda, but rather to educate about female-male sexual preferences without a bias.

The biggest issue and the holy grail for an incel is finding a way to make himself more attractive to women. As mentioned, these men go to great lengths to build their bodies, improve themselves, whilst still failing to find romance.

This is because women overwhelmingly value tall guys with handsome faces, who have social status, and money. "Personality" also plays a role, but the function of that characteristic in courtship is a little more complicated.

In our current competitive mating market, all attributes are considered when selecting a partner, and because of this, the incel is consistently left behind. This is because he suffers from a double-whammy of unattractiveness: he is both physically unattractive and, because his personality is in shambles from being insecure and unconfident, he is also socially inept. In short: he doesn't have the looks, and because he knows he doesn't have the looks, he doesn't have the personality either.

Human sexuality as a whole can be upsetting and create endless misery as we do not have much choice over who we find attractive or not. This chapter will summarize the blackpill literature which discusses the attributes women find attractive, and will then use this information to describe why incels continue to struggle romantically.

---

## Is It All About the Face?

---

Facial beauty has various dimensions. It is challenging to explain, with total clarity, what is considered to be a 'handsome' face.

This section is operating under the assumption that it is a near impossible task to perfectly define what makes a person's face 'attractive'. Perhaps this is because beauty cannot be defined.

Steven Weinberg writes, in *Dreams of a Final Theory: The Fundamental Laws of Nature* (1993):

> "I will not try to define beauty, any more than I would try to define love or fear. You do not define these things; you know them when you feel them."

Facial beauty is a seemingly, mystifying aesthetic trait. As such, an objective, operable standard definition will not be provided here.

There are voluminous pages written on facial aesthetics that add to the age-old debate of what is considered 'beautiful'.[1] Therefore, the view that there are universal judgments of facial beauty or of ideal facial proportions, will be not be the focus.

We will instead focus on the other end of the spectrum. This section will emphasize the consequences of being considered 'ugly', which result from intuitive judgements we place upon those we do not qualify as facially beautiful.

To stress this again, the human perception of "attractiveness" does not come from conscious reasoning. To the contrary: there is no clear conscious explanation for the preferences of one face to another. And unfortunately, as a result of this instinctive judgment, many individuals suffer emotionally, socially, and mentally.

In perhaps the most comprehensive and critical examination of facial aesthetics, Farhad Naini[2] expresses that facial proportions are fundamental to life and overall health.

Figure 4.2  Physical health, mental health and social well-being are all necessary requirements for overall health. In terms of the craniofacial region, examples of important functional parameters are visual and auditory, naso-respiratory, mastication, deglutition and phonation. Facial aesthetics is a requirement for mental health. All factors contribute to the health-related quality of life (HRQOL).

This might explain why facial surgery is becoming increasingly popular – a pretty face enhances one's quality of life.

One study[3] assessed the impact of facial aesthetics and reconstructive surgeries on enhancing self-confidence. The results revealed that facial aesthetic and reconstructive surgeries favorably affected the body image perception and self-esteem of the those who go under the knife.

Who knew that being appalled when you look at the mirror is not good for you? Shocking.

Notably, the authors of this study suggest that facial surgeries lead to better health because the patient starts to feel more confident on his own. Interestingly, this newfound confidence is not *only* internal, but mostly external.

When a dude's face is attractive, women are more interested. He is more desirable. He has a better chance at genuine intimacy and romance with women. He no longer has to pay for escort sex. *This* is what boosts his self-esteem and bolsters his mental health.

Being ugly messes with the mind. Humans, both men and women and everything in between, are social animals who want to be valued and appreciated by other humans.

We gain a lot of self-worth from how we are treated by our peers. If your face is ugly, it is going to mess with this. Imagine a community mistreating or even shunning you because of a few millimeters of facial bones beyond your control? Would you feel down? Depressed?

Based on a wide range of research, facial attractiveness is a strong indicator of fitness, health, and reproductive value.[4]

The preferences humans have for certain faces affects a range of critical social outcomes: popularity, mating choices, and platonic relationships. [5] Women judge and treat men as equally as men treat and judge women when it comes to attractiveness[6], suggesting that how we look is of primary importance for both sexes.

Moreover, when it comes to socio-economic standing, facial aesthetics matter, for both women and men. And this is impactful throughout one's employment history.[7]

It bears noting that there are more attractive women than attractive men: scientific evidence confirms the condition is slowly unraveling due to female-specific genetic traits and enhanced natural selection.[8]

Using data from both the National Longitudinal Study of Adolescent Health (Add Health) in the United States and the National Child Development Study (NCDS) in the United Kingdom, author Satoshi Kanazawa confirms:

> "If beautiful parents are more likely to have daughters, and if physical attractiveness is heritable (such that beautiful parents beget beautiful children and ugly parents beget ugly children), then it logically follows that, over many generations in the course of human evolution, the average level of physical attractiveness among women should gradually increase and the average level of physical attractiveness among men should gradually decrease. No matter what the initial sex difference in physical attractiveness (whether men were more attractive than women, women were more attractive than men, or there were no sex

differences in physical attractiveness), given long enough time, the outcome should be that women are on average more physically attractive than men are."

Moreover, in comparing facial and bodily attractiveness, at least one study has concluded that facial attractiveness is more important than the latter when people make judgments about overall physical attractiveness.

The results of the same study[9] concluded that, though bodily physique is an important factor in how both sexes determine overall physical desirability, the face is *more* valuable.

In an era where other forms of discrimination are especially prevalent, height discrimination can be overlooked and, at times, dismissed completely. The next section will explain the appeal of taller men and the resulting anxiety and feelings of inadequacy which is faced by shorter men in the mating market.

## THE IMPORTANCE OF BEING TALL

What is it about being tall? Evolutively speaking, we could contend that height is favored because tall people are characteristically larger, stronger, and therefore better equipped to protect their family from intruders. But a person's height does not necessarily indicate strength, speed, or fighting ability – so height should not afford any exceptionally distinctive advantage.

When it comes to this protector argument, plenty of short people exist whose overall weight and muscularity overshadow that of many taller individuals.

Possibly at the subconscious level, the logic follows, taller might just *seem* stronger or more capable because we associate height with power and strength. But are there voluntary or practical reasons for a height preference?

On a conscious level, most of us probably do not believe that we treat tall people any differently from short people. But there is plenty of evidence to suggest that height, does trigger a certain set of positive, unconscious connotations.

Unfortunately, at an overwhelming rate, study after study adds to the indignity of short people – or specifically short men.

The height of a potential partner matters more to women than to men, and predominantly because of matters of "femininity" and "protection."[10] This is a problem that women do not face.

On the whole, men find short girls just as desirable as tall ones. Short men, instead, are seen as less attractive and seemingly worse in every way, according to research.

Taller men have more economic and social success.[11] They are more likely to have children,[12] long-term relationships.[13] They are also more likely to have multiple long-term relationships,[14] and even second families.[15]

Only 14.5% of American men are 6 feet tall or taller and about 3% are taller than 6 feet 2 inches. But remarkably, 58% of CEOs of Fortune 500 companies in the United States are over 6 feet tall.[16]

The average height of all United States presidents is 5 feet 11 inches tall (average height for men in the United States is a little over 5 feet 9 ½ inches).

Americans are apparently captivated by the height of our future leaders. Google reported during the Republican debates for the 2016 election, that the top searched phrase had nothing to do with the debates' topics or policy issues. It was height-related. Specifically, the question: "How tall is Jeb Bush?"[17]

Undeniably, women (and men for that matter) seem to have a preference for taller men. One project[18], for instance, discovered that among 650 heterosexual college students, women largely preferred taller men and did not want to be in a relationship with a man shorter than they were.

In an Implicit Association Test (~1700 sample size[19]) it was found that there is a height bias where the very idea of a tall person is associated with positive traits such as moral goodness, wealth, and power.

Further: a national review conducted in the United Kingdom[20] found that shorter men made less money as a result of their height. It also found that a woman's height did *not* affect her pay (although there was an income difference associated with weight).

Moreover, research from Duke University,[21] determined that for every inch-below 5 feet 10 inches tall a man is, he must earn $40,000 more per year to be found as attractive as tall men.

Even sperm banks, typically, require men be at least 5 feet 8 inches tall.

The conclusion, there is an obvious basic standard that men *should* be taller – this is an idea that has been around for years. While it may *feel* natural to innately prefer a taller man over a shorter man, it is important to question where these preferences originated. Maybe there is a larger narrative at work?

Napoleon Bonaparte, according to legend, compensated for his lack of height by being a real dickhead to everyone and anyone. The man displayed an overly-aggressive and authoritarian attitude, simply because he was short.

As a result, the term 'Napoleon Complex', coined by Alfred Adler in 1926, was used to describe the perception of an inferiority complex about height. To put it simply, the term suggests that a shorter person's aggressive behavior is an overcompensation for their size.

But research challenges this stereotype of short, angry, aggressive people. A study[22] designed to test the "short man syndrome" found that taller men were more likely to lose their tempers. In other words, the results indicated that the 'Napoleon Complex' was a myth. And yet popular perception still associates shortness with anger and aggression.

Short men are undoubtedly discounted by many assortative mating preferences. This is especially evident in observed online dating behavior.

The dating website, Badoo, analyzed the "About Me" sections of their user base, taking note of the words used most commonly in these sections. As indicated by the list[23], the top ten most successful profiles repeated certain words more often than others. Notice the difference between the men's and women's preferences.

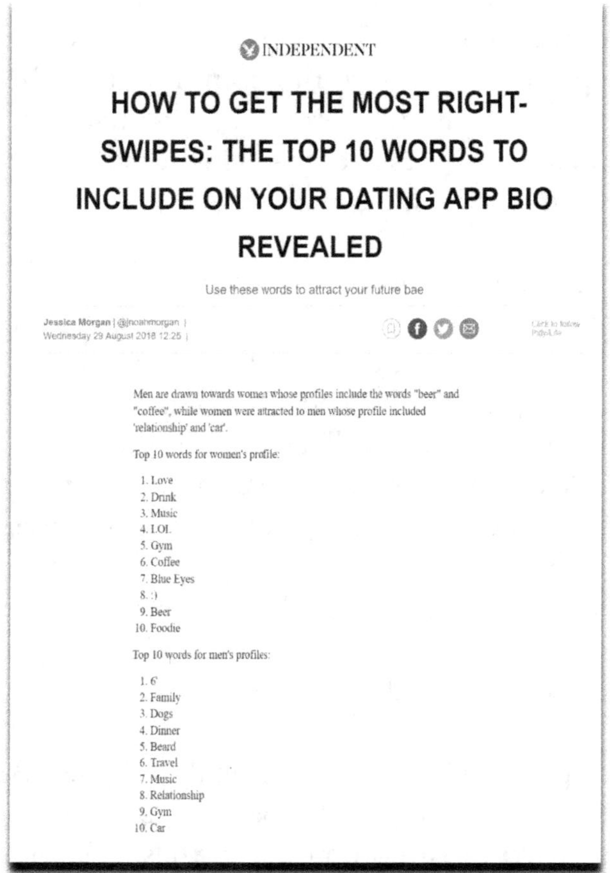

Ironically, it is actually men who say they want to "live, laugh, love", while women want a well-traveled, bearded man who is at least 6-feet tall and muscled, has a car, and is interested in dinner dates.

Of course, any man under 6-feet tall – cannot exactly meet the #1 listed trait – without flat out lying.

For the shorter man, it can be both revealing and sad to know how important the size of a man's skull and length of his limbs are to women. Because these are unchangeable physical traits. According to this data set, a man's height is literally more important than anything else about him.

But what is it about being six feet tall, specifically, that is so appealing to many women? A safe assumption would be to suggest that "6-foot height" symbolizes a status indicator for online women daters.

Think about it. A woman's arousal could still be reached physiologically or psychologically by a man, who stands far short of the arbitrarily preferred measurement height of six feet.

If measurement systems never existed, a numerical item would never be assigned next to the online height profile, and this massive filtering out of shorter men would not be the reality.

Before his personality or body or career is even considered, this arbitrary number filters out roughly 85% of men who fall below the 6-foot height threshold. These men are just not valuable to the women who have a height preference.

Why does this preference exist? We can conclude it is supported out of two things and two things only: arbitrary measurement systems and the inborn proclivities of some (*not* all) women to find a tall partner.

Those who disagree with this may put forth anecdotal rebuttals to what is being presented here. Stories such as, "I know several short men who date hot girls all the time!"

This does not disprove anything. Two, or five, or even 10,000 examples of short men who are attractive and successful will not disprove anything. The overwhelming overall trend is that taller is still better.

Human beings, both women *and* men, look to taller men for leadership. A man's tallness indicates that he has power, strength, and comes from a healthy gene pool. This is proven across sociological and behavioral psychological research. Our animal brains, which control visceral reactions, look to taller men as group leaders, which in turn makes them attractive to women. This is a documented tendency.

This does not mean that short men are worthless or completely hideous, and it does not mean that a taller guy will have hordes of women swiping on Bumble waiting to undress him as soon as the match is procured.

There are *many* other factors which contribute to how couples come together. However, dating is a process that is full of biases. Each individual, man or woman, brings their biases and preferences into the dating realm – even if they tell themselves they are open to anything.

The argument here is not that all women *only* prefer tall men – this would be a gross generalization. Instead, what is being offered is the observation that, according to a broad range of data, height is *one* of the most agreed upon an attractive trait, if not the most "attractive" trait in a man

---

## JUST BE CONFIDENT BRO (PERSONALITY/INTELLIGENCE)

---

At this point, many readers might still be denying the idea that "looks determine your life." Even incels might be doubting themselves; they might ask: what if my personality is being restricted by the emotions I have about myself and my appearance?

What if these emotions and anxieties and hang-ups *are* my personality?

The truth is, PERSONALITY DOES MEAN SOMETHING. This is true especially in terms of being charismatic, smart, charming, or neurotypical.

We are constantly told that these personality traits are attractive. But here's the catch: these qualities are much easier to acquire when one *is already attractive.* If you go through adolescence feeling ugly, and bullied, and depressed or like an outsider, a winning personality is harder to develop.

These preferred personality traits – charisma, a comfortable manner with others – are easier to develop when you grow up without feeling outcasted or marginalized. And it is easier to avoid these feelings if you are of average or above attractiveness.

A self-identified incel describes his experiences:

> "It's not because of me being self-conscious, it's about other people dismissing me because of my bad looks. If I had good looks, that never would have happened and my personality might not have suffered because of it. It all comes back around to looks, like everything else."

If a person is self-conscious about being ugly, they will act accordingly to that real or perceived perception and sabotage the chance of any real connection. They will be more likely to act nervous or anxious, and to be received as antisocial or distant. This is a feedback loop.

To be clear: this is not a rule. Many people with below-average attractiveness can get along just fine, developing attractive personalities and healthy social relations.

The argument here is that, on the whole, this is harder to do. More likely, an unattractive person will face an uphill battle, and will let their low self-esteem about their looks affect their ability to communicate and socialize.

So, the mantra, "looks determine your life" is only part of the blackpill. The other is that *personality will indeed attract women*, but not the kind of personality traits one would commonly think.

As it turns out, anti-social and exploitative adolescent bullies have more sex than others.[24] Adolescent bullies also have higher self-esteem and social status, more dating opportunities, and more sex when they get older.[25]

From an evolutive perspective, these collective traits might indicate that the most aggressive adolescents are the ones with the greatest sex appeal.

Testosterone stimulates aggression and general anti-social behavior.[26] It also promotes all the qualities that many women desire: height, dick size, masculine facial features, low body fat, and muscularity.[27] Coincidentally, there is evidence that testosterone levels are higher in violent and aggressive individuals.[28]

Following the theme, research has revealed that unempathetic, narcissistic, Machiavellian (dark triad) men – in short, assholes – are more attractive to women than those without those personality traits.[29]

One leads to the other – it does not matter which way you draw the arrow. These traits are an indicator for women who have either evolved to find it attractive or who have evolved to find the masculine looks associated with it attractive.

A prime example is Jeremy Meeks – the living embodiment of the blackpill.

The screen capture from Facebook shows four men, who were all arrested for the same crime, yet only Meeks went viral and became rich and famous as a result. Before his fame, he also had a career as a model, he was married, and had a child.

Being covered in gang tattoos, having multiple stints in prison, abandoning a child, and beating someone nearly to death did not stop him from finding a relationship. Must have been his charming personality, eh?

It is one of the more fascinating things about society: we convince ourselves that sexuality is wholesome and civil – rational and entirely *conscious* endeavor. It is not.

The absurdity sets in when it is thought about cogently: a few millimeters of facial and skull bones can change everything about life. Talent, kindness, generosity, courage – these are less important than bone structure, height, and testosterone levels.

As mentioned, the common suggestions offered to men who struggle to find dates or sex or relationships is oftentimes just to simply, "improve your personality." This advice implies incorrect assumptions: 1) men who are romantically unsuccessful have bad personalities, and 2) men who are romantically successful have good personalities.

Take a second to think about the single men in your community, social network, or family. Many of them likely do have nice or caring personalities. They might even possess certain personality traits which many women claim to find attractive: sense of humor, kindness, intelligence, compassion, and generosity. And despite all these positive qualities, they still fall endlessly with the opposite sex.

On the flip side, millions of men with objectively bad personalities (as noted previously) find love, sex, and fulfillment with women every single day.

These romantically successful men are seen as better and more ethical, while the romantic failures are seen as defective and dangerous. This can even compound upon itself as women find men who are desired by other women to be even more attractive[30] (this effect did not extend to men looking at paired women).[31]

The fundamental error people make is mistaking sexual selection for a moral or ethical judgement or for anything other than what it is — a selection based on genetic fitness for reproduction.

One of the most brutal uncovered truths over several mediums of research was that, in most cases, a man must meet a minimum looks threshold before his personality is even considered.

Consider the conclusions of the following study:

> "Men with the most desirable personality profiles were rated more favorably than their counterparts only when they were at least moderately attractive. Unattractive men were never rated as more desirable partners for daughters, even when they possessed the most desirable trait profiles."[32]

We can also find a similar effect with intelligence. Yes, being smart matters to a degree, but usually after one has passed the looks test.

With that said, keep in mind that even if a man does pass the minimum looks test and the woman suddenly gets to appreciate how smart or narcissistic he is, there are millions of other guys out there who are far better looking that he will be competing with.

Nevertheless: personality does matter.

While the data is discouraging, it does not spell total doom for men below the attractiveness threshold. The other side of the coin, which incels too seldom admit, is the fact that positive mental traits do influence desirability.[33] The question is just to what degree.

There is an evolutionary basis for mental attributes having an effect on sexual attraction. For instance, it would make sense to choose a highly intelligent, or profoundly talented, self-assured partner.

Even a handsome man who also happens to be cognitively weak can possess skill-sets which tend to be less valuable to society. They are poorer strategists, they're habitually exploited, and ultimately cannot provide as much value as those who mentally dominate them.

These factors certainly bolster the idea that intelligence can sometimes overcome looks. However, in the most formative years of a man's sexual life, intellect and acumen are not as practical in earning attention from the opposite sex. Younger boys of course live with their parents and will not put their cerebral talents to use for years.

Adolescents have little to show for their intelligence besides good grades – they do not own businesses, they have not built material or social capital with their acumen. Because mental fitness is less of a factor in these school years, the rewards adolescent men receive from the opposite sex for their intellectual abilities are minimal.

So, in these key years, physicality far outweighs intellect and intelligence in its ability to attract adolescent women.

The unfortunate side of this, which must be stressed, is that youth is a series of feedback loops which establishes "confidence" in oneself. If a boy is more athletic, and treated better for his stunning physical attractiveness and superiority, he is most likely going to develop a high level of confidence.

His confidence is a valuable social tool, which in turn makes him more attractive to others. So, the physical attractiveness feeds the personality's attractiveness, and vice versa.

This works on the opposite side of the spectrum, too. Inferior social skills are strongly linked to unattractiveness or other negative physical traits. More often than not, you won't have one without the other.

Although looks are the primary focus in the online communities, some incels do admit that they might be "mental-cels" acknowledging that their personality or their autism is what is holding them back from being successful with women.

We even have research[34] confirming that 'mental-cels' struggle in the same way high-functioning autistic adolescents struggle when it comes to relationships. 69% of adolescents with high-functioning autism spectrum disorder (ASD) desired a girlfriend, or a marriage, or a family but almost none succeeded. Moreover, 44.6% of autistic men remain virgins, despite having a normal drive for sex and a relationship.[35]

And sadly, since suicidal thoughts are linked to greater autistic traits, there may be a direct link between ASD and suicidal behavior. Men with Asperger's syndrome have ten times as many suicidal thoughts as men who do not.[36]

A self-identifying incel writes:

> "I dream and plan about suicide every day. I've always thought about suicide, but it has never been this frequent and this serious. I don't even feel emotional. I think it's pretty much impossible for me to be happy, it's pointless to keep living at this point. I ~~tries~~ [*sic*] everything I can for years. Literally every kind of self-improvement you can ever think of. Including a surgery. No matter how hard I try, no matter what I do, I always lose. I was very hopeful about the future when I was a kid, a delusion of grandeur. I guess I am going to slit my wrists and wait for death, as far as I know that's a painless way to go. I don't know what else to say. Everything became

meaningless. I don't even want anything at all. I stopped eating, I stopped going to gym, lost around 15 kgs. in about a week. My dick stopped working. I don't have a desire for anything. It's the end of the journey I guess. So, that's how my life ends. That's how my story ends. I wish it hadn't been like this."

Humans are, to a large degree, tools for a functioning society. We need to be *functional* in order to feel like we are part of the world, necessary in some way to others. Broken tools are useless, however, and many incels are broken.

It was mentioned earlier in the book, but the alarming suicide rates (for both sexes) are not something we discuss enough. For reference, since 1999 the suicide rate has climbed by 33%.[37] At the societal level, this is both a puzzling and concerning trend. Depression seems to be the most important potential risk for suicide and suicidal thoughts.

In summary, this section cites several reasons to explain the degree in which personality does "matter."

The point has been made numerous times now, but evidence suggests women are in search of optimal partners, at least on dating apps. And today, the dating app is the primary way individuals are searching for a mate. This will all be elaborated upon in Chapter VI.

Nonetheless, the argument here, considering all relevant research is that poor looks preclude a man from obtaining sex more often than a poor personality because looks are more easily judged.

Snap judgments about looks allow the opposite sex to quickly narrow their options – it is an efficient evolutionary technique for choosing partners. This does not doom the unattractive to a totally sexless life. But it does set them back in their quest for sex, love, and intimacy.

When we first encounter someone, what is it that we see first? What they look like. This is why a charismatic, charming, and funny incel can be ruled out of many potential relationships before a single word is exchanged.

No one possesses the extrasensory perception to recognize the entire character of an individual right off the bat. Which means that an ugly man can have the most amazing personality imaginable, but he will not be able to showcase it because women will reject him on sight. How do you get to know someone who is not willing to get to know you?

Overtime, of course, a woman could determine that a man does meet her personality standards — but the incredible natural demand for each and every woman means that she probably will not need to settle for a man with a great personality but minimal physical attractiveness. Generally speaking, she can instead wait for someone who has both.

To describe this section in terms of the blackpill, personality has no biological value. Animals do not pick a breeding or mating partner based off of "personality," which is why it is evolutively less valuable than looks.

## I Ain't Sayin' She's a Gold-digger

One of the most widely accepted formulae in American society is that wealth equals success. This is instilled in us by our family, our teachers, the mass media, and our social interactions throughout life.

Despite its significance, money is, after all, a social construct made up by people. As such, the key question when it comes to evaluating monetary value is the following: can an artificially assigned social rank determine an individual's romantic success over nature's metric for determining a mate's value (looks)?

Under the blackpill, attractiveness holds far more sway over sexual outcomes than does monetary success – this is because attractiveness is a purely biological trait.

In the past men would happily be the breadwinner because it would ensure them a wife and family, but this is no longer a reality. In modern society, women earn their own money and provide for themselves – this has been the case for decades in the United States.

In terms of men (or PUAs) who follow the redpill, it is common to emphasize ideals of "money" and "status" because money and status seem achievable through effort, at least in contrast to replacing one's facial bones.

These men observe a naturally hot, sexy dude getting loads of attention from several women. Instead of believing that this attention is largely due to the man's looks – they argue that its due to "status" or "game" or "being an alpha." They believe that the factors involved are under their control.

Redpillers like to repeat these sunshiny mantras because it helps them cope and feel better. For the redpiller, "game" and behaving like an "alpha" are all behaviors that can be learned through study and practice. With just a little effort, he can draw as much attention from women as the hot dude.

With that noted, for all the hate the redpill receives when it comes to sexual strategy, it does keep men motivated and productive.    In contrast, the increasing numbers of men becoming blackpilled, can lead to demotivation and a "check-out" from society.

As mentioned at the opening of the book, more and more men (both incels and non-incels) are coming to the decision that no matter what they do, they will never be good enough, so they have stopped even trying.

The key driver here is men becoming increasingly likely to question the motivations of both women and societal institutions, with the implication that these men lose more faith with each examination.

Moving forward, if these trends continue, frugality will be more common. Who needs a fancy, new car? A stylish expensive wardrobe? A nebulous career?

The economy we currently have could take huge hits if men stopped buying expensive shit to impress women. Five-star restaurants fold. Flower businesses fail. Jewelry stores close their doors and the value of commodities like gold and diamonds plummets. The wedding industry is already suffering. Our society requires a large population of productive individuals and spenders to keep civilization spinning – knock out large sections of them and what happens?

With that said, incel detractors often cite conventionally unattractive men as rebuttals to the above – "I see ugly dudes with girlfriends all the time!" Although this claim is certainly true, from what is being observed, the majority of incels do not want to be "settled for" due to their financial status. Because they are mindful of having been completely ignored when they were younger.

As such, incels have a gloomy distrust of money as a factor in dating. Those who are financially successful fear that any interested woman is only interested in their money.

A common questioning series posed in the incel community would be the following: Would she have dated me when she was younger? Would she have given me the time of the day back then? Why now?

Time and time again incels conclude that it's solely the woman's financial circumstances that have led her to consider the incel as a dating prospect, after ignoring him for the majority of her teens and twenties. Incels find this situation untenable. They would rather die alone than be "settled" for. Remember: the core desire of most incels is not a trophy or an empty sexual relationship – it is intimacy and love.

Incels do not have a solution to these despondent feelings. And there will never be one if the general public does not recognize that this entire situation is a real problem – at both the individual and societal levels.

Examples of the "ugly guy with hot girl" meme is partly why the incel declaration that "looks are everything" is not universally accepted and can be so vehemently attacked. And this meme does have some merit, because remember, evolutively speaking, women are at least partially attracted to men who can provide.

The notion of women being attracted to a man's status is generally accepted across several sociological studies. It is also incentivizing for the man to maintain a higher earning position throughout the relationship because if he clears less money than his wife, the marriage is more likely to dissolve.[38] This is becoming an increasingly common trend as approximately 38% of wives earn more than their husbands, according to the Bureau of Labor Statistics.

Women are outperforming men, across a wide range of measures, which is explained in further detail in the next section. They graduate at much higher rates, are more likely to attend graduate school, and single women out-earn single men.

As for the other side, according to the Bureau of Labor Statistics, over 11% of men between the ages of 25 and 54 (around 7 million people) were unemployed or seeking employment. The gloomy state of prime-age men is alarming.

Many experts are attempting to explain the current predicament. But, as far as I know, no one is offering a genuine interest into the mind of the sexless, lonely, and romantically unwanted for an explanation.

With that noted, one possible reason women are more selective now is that, with divorces and infidelity becoming so common, it is too risky to take unmotivated men as partners. Plus, if a woman is earning her own money, she no longer needs to rely on the financial provider. Accordingly, women have more freedom to be more selective with physical traits when it comes to choosing a partner.

## DUAL MATING STRATEGY & HYPERGAMY

Ever wondered why nearly all the media we consume features ugly, unpopular "nerds" and attractive, popular "jocks"? These blackpills are literally shoved down our throats from early childhood by television and movies.

Despite these countless portrayals and images, the majority of people refuse to accept the power of our looks. Why? Society needs to keep the hope alive, dude. Because without hope, men give up, they began to check out, stop working, and put little effort into attracting women. That *hope* keeps society spinning and civilization turning.

For this reason, a lot of men go to school, earn advanced degrees, get well-paying jobs with the *hope* that he will achieve a status and an income that is attractive to women. And there is nothing wrong with this ideal; having dedication and passion towards a career is not only attractive, but gratifying and fulfilling.

Universally and disproportionately women consider a man's earning potential as a criterion for dateability and marriageability.

A girl desiring a man for what can be provided hypothetically sounds like a good thing for an unattractive man, right? Well, not exactly.

For right or wrong, under a blackpill guise this situation is problematic, despite the evidence that plain, average-looking men end up in marriages all the time. These relationships are actually evidence for the blackpill, as these men are "beta bucks."

A beta bucks is slang for a man whose relationship with his girlfriend or wife hinges (although both parties deny it) entirely on his ability to provide for her preferred lifestyle. This is not a genuine physical attraction but a transactional relationship based on the resources which can be provided.

Overall, this type of attraction is fine and it does work if one can achieve such a level in his profession where he can provide in such a way.

The issue here is twofold for the incel:

1) As mentioned previously, most incels do not only want sex. If they did they could just pay for it. No: they want what they would presume to be a non-transactional relationship, a relationship where the other person likes them for them—and that is not a reality for the vast majority of people, especially unattractive ones.

Very rich, but out-of-shape and unattractive men have a relatively easy time getting interest from women, but they cannot make a woman genuinely desire to have sec with them on a physical level – it is just the very commercial version of negotiating desire.

If you are considered an ATM, this is seen as a bogus relationship – which incels overwhelmingly do not want. In this way, incels are like most other people. There are few people who would feel healthy and satisfied in such a transactional relationship.

2) It takes an unbelievable amount of willpower and determination – and usually a lot of luck –  to be successful. This extreme resolve and discipline just isn't present today in males, in general, and especially not in incels.

So many young men do not show any determination because they do not see much hope of ever succeeding in society. The standards and expectations are overwhelming, and few people actually succeed unless they start from a point of advantage. As a consequence, these young men opt to give into despair.

Women need men less today than they ever have in history, especially in wealthy countries – such as the United States. The so-called American Dream is not disappearing merely because of financial inequality, but also because of emotional and romantic inequality.

Of course, most incels have at some point in time wanted a great career, a nice house, a loving relationship with a girlfriend or wife, and close male friendships.  But circumstances are such that these basic features of "the good life" are becoming very hard to achieve.

Take this quote from an incel posted on reddit as an illustration:

> "I never started out as a lonely virgin who makes bitter posts to a lonely virgin subreddit and lambasts foids [females] all the time. Nor did I actively make lifestyle choices that led me down this path. You know what I wanted to do for the longest time, my ultimate goal in life? I wanted to be a father to a child because I never had a father. I wanted a loving family that would support me and I would support them in return. I wanted to provide a stable family environment for my future children because I never had that luxury. Why, then, did I end up here? Because I am an ugly and short male. That is the ONLY reason. I was your stereotypical polite, respectful, and quiet person for the longest time. The world has stomped and spit on me because of my genetics and I became this way as a result. It was not the product of "toxic masculinity" or some other retarded shit. I

became a cynical shit-poster that hates life because society has shit on me. It infuriates me that cucks think they know what I or any other low-value male have been through."

This is quintessential blackpill logic.

The mating market is highly competitive, and the blackpiller argues that "average" as a man is just not good enough. Due to a variety of factors mentioned above, opportunities are shrinking overall despite the ideal that society has evolved to require men to prove their worth.

The standard for men is obsolete, it belongs to a different time period and context. But it is still being held as the standard. In fact, men have very few clear ways to prove their worth in today's day and age. They are suffering humiliation and checking out, precisely because they are not meeting a standard that has become unattainable and unreal.

And even IF incels do improve to a level of attaining a loving relationship, there seems to be an overwhelming sentiment to avoid marriage amongst the group.

Helen Smith (Ph.D.), author of "Men on Strike," perhaps summarizes the overall incel reaction towards marriage best:

> "Men know there's a good chance they'll lose their friends, their respect, their space, their sex life, their money and — if it all goes wrong — their family. They don't want to enter into a legal contract with someone who could effectively take half their savings, pension and property when the honeymoon period is over. Men aren't wimping out by staying unmarried or being commitment phobes. They're being smart."

This leaves quite the dilemma for the man who is starting from genetically as 2/10 in the looks department – is self-improvement even worth it considering all the risks involved? Is it "being smart" to just give up and check out?

Undeniably, marriage is just not as popular as it used to be. In fact, according to Jay L. Zagorsky

(Ph.D.), the marriage rate in the U.S. is the lowest it's been in at least 150 years.[39]

One explanation, as concluded by a recent study,[40] is that there are not enough "economically-attractive" available men that single women want to marry. In an interview with Yahoo Lifestyle[41], the study's lead researcher, Daniel T. Lichter (Ph.D.) added:

> "Economic stability is a key to a stable family life — to getting married, staying married, and marrying well," he says. "Physical attractiveness may provide an initial filter that draws our attention, but economic considerations and shared values matter much more in the long term. A good job attracts and retains suitable marital partners. And this is true for both men and women."

Lichter goes on to add that "finding potential male partners who are economically secure may not matter as much when women are the financially-secure ones." Both comments overwhelmingly support the blackpill.

It is a widespread precondition of a women's happiness that the man with whom she is sexually involved be financially secure, at least after the initial filter of physical attractiveness has been met.

Love and affection is just simply not enough for a suitable marital partner. Looks and financial security are also required.

Which leads us to a discussion of the following, controversial, evolutionary psychological observational theory: women have a duplicitous mating strategy. The following, according to popular belief across the manosphere, is the dual biological imperative of what women are attracted to:

1. physical attraction (genes)
2. life comforts (resources)

When writers in the manosphere discuss "Alpha Fucks, Beta Bucks" this is essentially the dynamic they are referring too.

In essence, the formula is this: want one (or multiple) guys to have sex with, and someone else to provide the commitment and life resources. Or, in rare cases and only for the most desirable women, the same guy who fulfills both needs.

Most attention is focused on the beta bucks (the bluepill) side of the attraction dynamic. This allows the nicer, nerdier men an opportunity to provide the life comforts through a well-paid career.

In theory, this does not sound like a bad opportunity for the incel: study hard, land a good job, then find a woman who will be attracted to the comforts and stability your career can provide to her. But in practice, she does not desire him sexually, even though she still does want him – to be her provider, her economic utility.

In other words, the theory posits that women are attracted to both men who are physically superior and experienced (alpha fucks) but also simultaneously seek to secure a man who is incredibly loyal and will provide for her (beta bucks).

It is very difficult to find both in one man because often times the alpha guy is a risky gamble – she is physically attracted to him but at the same time is also unsure if he will ever be "marriage material."

In other words, the traits that make a man a good sexual partner to women sometimes make him a bad relationship partner.

As mentioned previously, this duality is very rational. Selecting a partner to fall in "love" with based on good genes and abundant resources is a pragmatic decision.

Beyond their increased financial autonomy, other modern developments have increased women's power to determine their mates, and made them less hamstrung by limiting social and economic circumstances. Birth control afforded women increased power over their reproductive system and allowed them to run their pre-existing strategy more effectively. Beyond the Pill, this sexual strategy has also been facilitated by the advent of online dating apps.

Consider the declining sex chart again on the next page. There is only one reason that the number of sexless men can be increasing while the number of sexless women is constant: hypergamy. Given sexual freedom, women simply have little desire to have sex with the average or the below-average man.

The gap between the regular person's beliefs and this fact is so wide, and the implications are so horrifying to them, that their brains simply cannot even consider the idea.

It is fascinating, and often hilarious, to consider the sorts of explanations for observed data that one must invent when the obvious truth is forbidden from a socially approved ideology.

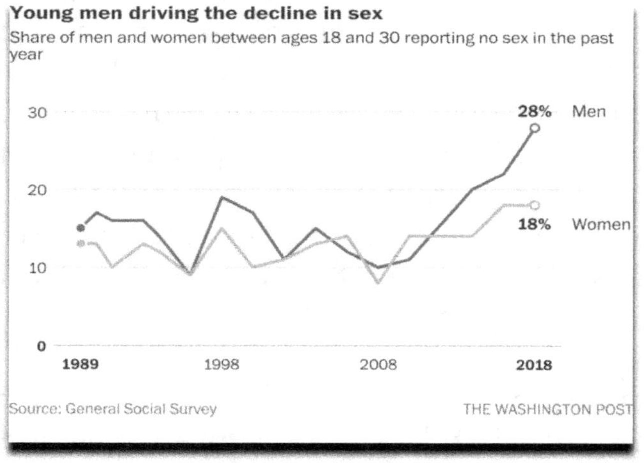


Like the early astronomers who derived complex orbits to explain the peculiar movements of planets in the solar system, the modern social scientist or journalist will create all sorts of absurd explanations for the rising number of men not having sex as the number of women having sex remains constant.

Delayed marriage! Labor force participation! Pornography! I somewhat expect them to suggest that it is because Mercury is in retrograde.

Anyways, most are probably wondering what exactly hypergamy is, so let's get into it. Hypergamy is an evolutionary psychological theory to explain the mating market. It essentially means that women tend to mate across and up hierarchies.

The illustration on the next page provides a sample framework of hypergamy in practice (the left-hand side represents men and the right-hand side represents women). Hypergamy has many selective styles of determining a quality mate.

It has been stated previously that the majority of women use a man's height as a physical qualification for attraction. It is one of the more obvious criteria — select the height box on a dating app, and move on to the harder stuff.

Empirical research on sexual selection and mate choices confirms hypergamy, too.

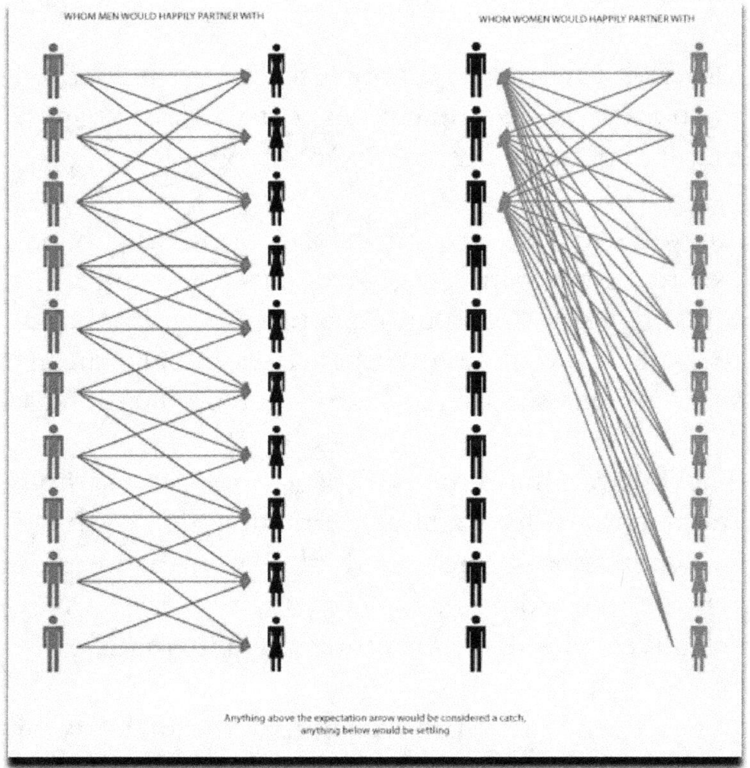


The full text of this article[42] is a great summary of the field (the .pdf will be linked in the notes). Honestly, the whole thing is thought-provoking and worth a read – here are a few selections relating to female sexual strategy:

> "In primate species in which long-term relationships develop, females generally prefer dominant males as mates. In comparison to other males, dominant males provide greater protection from conspecifics (i.e., members of the same species) and often provide better access to high-quality foods (Smuts, 1985). Similarly, the social status of men is an important consideration in women's choices of and preferences for marriage partners (Buss, 1994). Although the markers of social status can vary somewhat from one culture to the next (Irons, 1979, 1983), the basic relation is the same: Culturally successful men are preferred as mating and marriage partners."

(…)

> "Research conducted throughout the world strongly supports the position that women prefer marriage partners who are culturally successful or have the potential

to become culturally successful. The most extensive of these studies included 10,000 people in 37 cultures across six continents and five islands" (Buss, 1989).

(…)

"Across age, ethnic status, and socioeconomic status, women preferred husbands who were better educated than they were and who earned more money than they did. Buunk and colleagues found the same pattern for women ranging in age from their 20s to their 60s" (Buunk, Dijkstra, Fetchenhauer, & Kenrick, 2002).

(and lastly the summary and conclusions.)

"Although the details of how success is achieved can vary from one setting to the next, culturally successful men have high reproductive potential and high reproductive success" (Irons, 1979; Low, 2000).

"In short, most women prefer monogamous marriages to wealthy, socially dominant, and physically attractive men, and want these men to be devoted to them and their children. For most women, this preference is not achieved. Some women attempt to achieve a compromise of sorts through relationships with several men. The implicit goal appears to be to get the best material investment from one man and the best genetic investment from another."

There is plenty to digest in the article – including commentary on male mating strategies.

If the evolutionary science-y side of mating interpretation does not pique one's interest, the feminist media outlet, the *Huffington Post*, has written hypergamy-type articles too – it will be linked[43] as well.

A relevant quote from the *Huff Post* article:

"Naturally, we don't date the Bottom 10, and with good reason. Your personal Bottom 10 is a no-fly-zone. **If you feel repelled by someone, there is no overcoming that feeling, no matter how**

**great of a person he is**. If you've ever tried dating in your Bottom 10, you know how futile that is. He is not the guy for you."

After reading this chapter, I understand if anyone concludes that this is a very negativistic approach to the mating market and/or relationships.

There is no way to prove that all women are hypergamous. There are ways to observe trends through the lenses of sociology, evolutionary psychology, and biology, but it cannot be proven statistically.

To be certain, the tendencies and preferences described here exist in various degrees, and in some cases not at all, for each individual woman. What are being observed are general trends, biases and behaviors that apply to large swaths of the population. Many women may not at all operate according to these subconscious inclinations. But research shows that a large number of women do.

To summarize briefly, the blackpill asserts that looks are far more important than people generally believe. It does *not* argue that status or money (or even personality and intelligence) have zero effect. But, overall, looks determine mating opportunities more so than other attributes and female behavior and preferences, observed across a wide-range of scientific research, confirm this declaration.

# VI. DATING APPS

With today's prevalence of smartphones and apps, online dating has become more common than ever before — it has developed into part of our mainstream culture.

The popularity of online dating apps exploded with the launch of Tinder in 2012. But the breadth and diversity of online dating have expanded well beyond Tinder in the last few years.

There are niche dating apps for dog owners, conservatives, Christians, Bernie Sanders supporters, beard lovers, vegans, meat-eaters — the demand is so high that unique subgroups continue to be created and catered to.

Theoretically, no matter one's age, gender, or sexual preference, a man or woman can create the modern variant of the personal ad and post their profile online to connect with thousands of people within minutes.

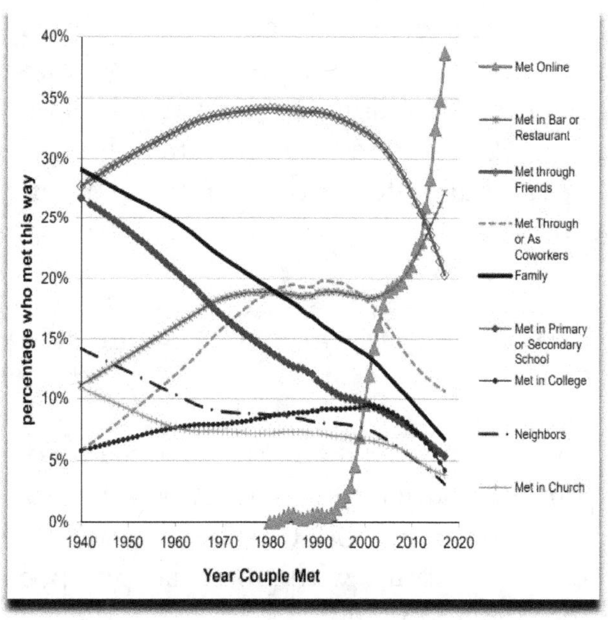



As indicated in the figure,[1] online dating has become the number one place for couples to meet, replacing meeting through friends or in a bar or restaurant.

Women and men are looking online for exciting potential matches that their real-life social networks do not offer.

For the most part, users scroll through people on their cell phones as if they are shopping online for new clothing. The profile biographies and criteria are largely the same (avid traveler, enjoy hiking, like to have fun, fluent in sarcasm, etc.) so many use openers after matching with lines that boil down to being fun and interesting; resulting in the same stock personality for most almost everyone you come across.

---

## "DATING APPS ARE NOT REAL LIFE!"

---

As shown, dating apps and other social medias are the primary outlets in which people do their partner searching, today. These resources are stocked to the brim with potential prospects for both women and men.

The initial contact between people – the foundation of these apps and websites – is based on surface level qualities because those are the only traits people can see at that point.

People like to claim that online dating behavior is "not the way people act in real life" and they are right!

Dating apps are realer than real life!

It is how people act when they know there are limited consequences and zero shame – their deepest instincts, their most honest feelings, and their most unabashed self-presentation, are all laid out for the world to see!

Across the board, online dating apps serve the same purpose. People love to claim that Tinder, as an example, is just for "hooking-up" but that is a weak assessment. Tinder is much more than an online speed dating event, it is a mainstream social scene.

Users intentions are highly varied and because of this variety, the app serves users in a variety of ways. In general, however, Tinder's role is help users meet attractive others who share similar interests and bring them under your social media umbrella.

This union of both dating app and social media is highlighted by the innovation of linking Instagram and Spotify profiles to one's Tinder profile. As an outcome, Tinder is not the secretive, private hook-up app as so many claim. It is for birthing new social media relationships, rather than maintenance of the relationships which already exist.  After the establishment of a match between two users, they become familiarized with one another's social life. From there on out, it feels just like meeting in real life.

From the preliminary profile impression, until whatever eventually emerges, human nature plays out just as expected in the real world. These dating apps do not alter innate human biology, they simply assist pre-existing tendencies. So, if the claim is that "Tinder is just a hook-up app", then all real-life meetings are too.

Above all, the vein of Tinder is simply to socialize with others who you find attractive. As will be uncovered, a man who is not attractive does not get to play.

Under a blackpilled lens, a significant percentage of men are being sexually selected against en masse —

which is verifiable by the fact that nearly 1/3 of men under the age of 30 are not having sex.

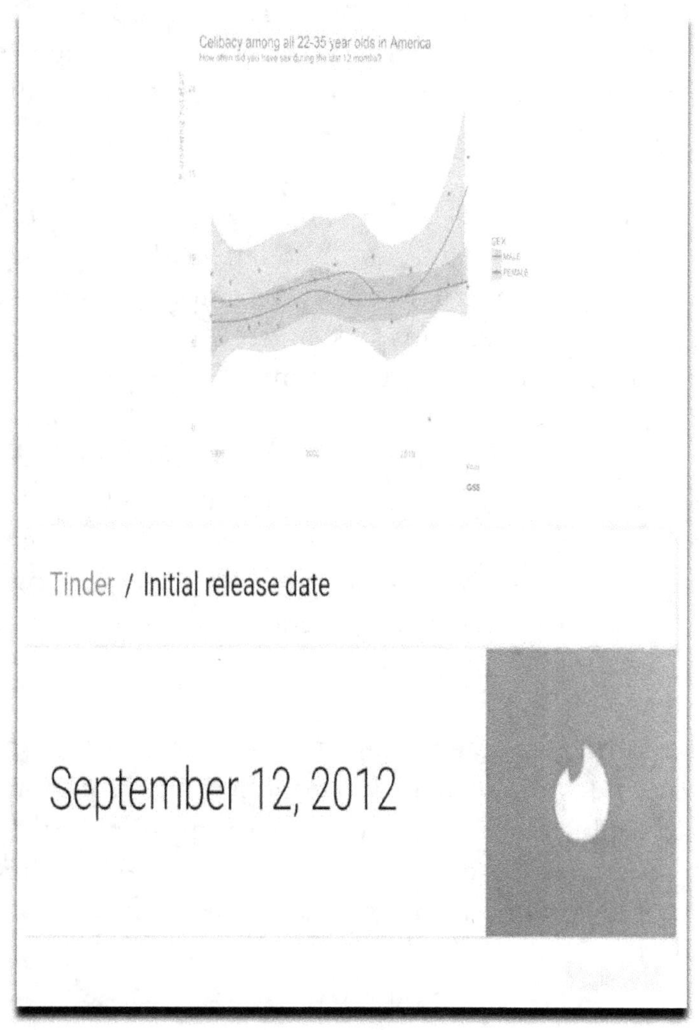

The rise in sexlessness aligns coincidentally with the release of Tinder in 2012.[2] The chart poses the question, "How often did you have sex during the last 12 months?" Notice the climb in "not at all" responses around 2012.

We can think of dating apps as similar to the current job market, as it relates to low-wage workers. There are so many unemployed people that an employer can pick and choose who they wish, even for part-time minimum wage jobs.

A company may be hiring for a 10 hour per week position, but still require the potentially employee to be fully flexible for the entire week – just in case. This less-than-desirable position might require two years of real world experience and a four-year degree.

The hiring manager might have a resume from someone with 7 years' experience and someone with only 4 years *plus* qualifications – and they obviously choose the latter. Why? Because they can. This is something we can all agree on.

We can, likewise, all agree that while businesses should avoid hiring practices such as this, they would be out of their minds not to, because the system allows it.

So, imagine all these potential lower wage workers out there competing against others who have better degrees, more qualifications, more experience, higher flexibility. The deck is well-stacked against them. And this is before an interview, where there is at least a slight opportunity to sell oneself as a hard worker with an easy-going personality.

Of course, there are several things one can do to come across as a better candidate than others once an interview is procured — a well-crafted resume, a sharp suit, a fresh haircut. But a person wearing rags and a poorly written resume with 10 years' experience will still be given more of a chance than the guy wearing rags and a poorly written resume with only 3 years' experience.

And, if by chance the job turns out to be yours, well the company can treat you badly because there is a long queue of other people who are willing and able to take it off your hands.

Once again, we hope companies would not exploit workers in this way, but they do. The system allows it. And our anger is at the system itself, not the employer.

How does this relate to dating apps and unattractive dudes?  Easily — just swap the job market for sexual mating market. Swap segments of the resume for physical characteristics — years of experience for facial symmetry, qualifications for height and muscularity, degrees as the "dating biography".  Swap getting an interview with getting a date and so on. Swap the job treating the employee negatively, knowing that the worker can be easily replaced, for a woman treating the man unenthusiastically, knowing that he can be easily replaced.

Yes, there are exceptions to the online dating rule. Yes, as will be determined below, it is not 100% exclusively about great looks and height.

Again, if a dude shows up in rags to a first date and has not showered in a month or declares on his resume or dating profile that he "likes to kick cats", he's not doing himself any favors.

But the more attractive cat-kicker is still going to be treated more fairly than the unattractive one.

Deep down we all agree that dating heavily weighs on physical attributes. Tinder and its massive success seem to prove this beyond a shadow of a doubt. But still, few people openly admit this.

Recall how it was established that we cannot blame the businesses for being picky and elitist? The same thing applies to dating and women. Women cannot be criticized for trying to get the best deal. It may be hard for incels to empathize with this. But if they were in any of these women's place, they would behave quite the same, trying to find the best option and bringing all their advantages to bear in doing so.

Incels are undoubtedly frustrated towards women (and often despicably so) but the true resentment is and should be directed toward the confusing and exclusive mating market we are all required to participate in.

## BLACKPILL & ONLINE DATING

The basic premise of blackpill online dating is that each and every physical trait of a man is significant and seldom disregarded by a woman when selecting for a match.

Searching or swiping for the right partner is in many ways similar to other important life-decisions like selecting a college or buying a new car. The key similarity in each of these scenarios is that decisions are ultimately made after a total analysis of attributes. Every individual characteristic, even tiny ones, can make a huge difference in one's degree of satisfaction and selection.

A gamer, for example, would not knowingly skimp by on resolution or a processer when buying a new computer. If he can afford it, he will always go with the one with both a vibrant display and processing power. Sacrifices are only made when absolutely necessary. In the sexual and dating market, females are of utmost demand and for this reason they are rarely desperate and can therefore be highly selective. As a result of this near unlimited currency, they do not need to make risky sacrifices or choices.

When females decide to go "window-shopping" for a serious or even casual partner, the product is always available. To stretch this metaphor, women can often afford to select the "deluxe" variety.

Of course, facial features, degree of fitness, pleasant skin, height, and other desirable physical traits are the attributes men would be putting on display in this online mating ritual.

An incel will not exactly have the advantage over other guys when it comes to physical attributes, but he can still be witty, interesting, and charming. To have a pleasant experience online the incelibate would need to overcome his genetic disadvantages and win matches with his personality – we can build a dating profile as a case study.

Of course, personality in this instance, is the featured trait for potential desirability, so the incels biography needs to sound both fun, exciting, and engaging. Stray too far from being "normal" and you are now "weird." Stray too far away from "pop culture" and you are now "boring."

Since your profile is so constrained by society's simplistic and narrow standards of what is weird or normal, exciting, or boring, the incel is forced to talk about the activities and hobbies that he partakes in. Sounds easy enough, right?

If he participates in activities that give off hints of being a loner – who video games, for instance – the woman might now question his social pedigree. This constraining problem now allows physical factors to have even more influence.

For the sake of discussion, let us assume an incel does eventually procure a match with a woman, after she wades through her pool of potential suitors. Remember, however, incels are not as physically gifted as their peers so the speech window will be limited once a conversation is established.

In other words, since incels are unattractive, the conversational stakes are higher. Say one dumb or awkward thing and he might not get another chance. Nerve-racking.

And we still live in a culture which suggests men

are supposed to lead the conversation and courtship

Of course, one would need to be establish a "normal" but impassioned – not "weird" or boring – conversation with a woman who has like five lines of dialogue.

"I like to travel, drink wine, and be with my dog!"

What is YOUR move? And this is just one of the dilemmas faced by the unattractive.

With the above noted, it is interesting then that the standard female mate selection procedure eliminates undesirable men right away. This is the first indication of the significance of aesthetic appearances in female-male courtship.

Consider the vast aggregate of all opportunities where one could find a date. This includes everything from bars to class or work to the park to online dating. In most of those situations you have an opportunity to put your personality out at the same time as your looks, showing perhaps that you exude confidence or charisma.

But these personality traits cannot necessarily be showcased online, so the judgements are almost all visual.

---

### "CHADFISHING"

---

Incels routinely complain that after considerable trials, even with unique well-written profiles and professional photographs, they have still completely failed to obtain any real online matches or genuine online connections. And if they do match, it rarely results in a real-life meetup.

However, when they design a more Chad-like profile[3], full of photos of an attractive random man with a square jaw and immaculately groomed stubble, a model they found on Instagram perhaps, they then become flooded with both matches and genuine interest.

Incels have even labelled this practice, "Chadfishing." Once a match is procured with the fake Chad, conversations flow with ease and women are more receptive to even blatant sexual advances.

There are numerous examples of this across the internet, but for illustration here is an example of a "Chadfish" and two sample interactions.

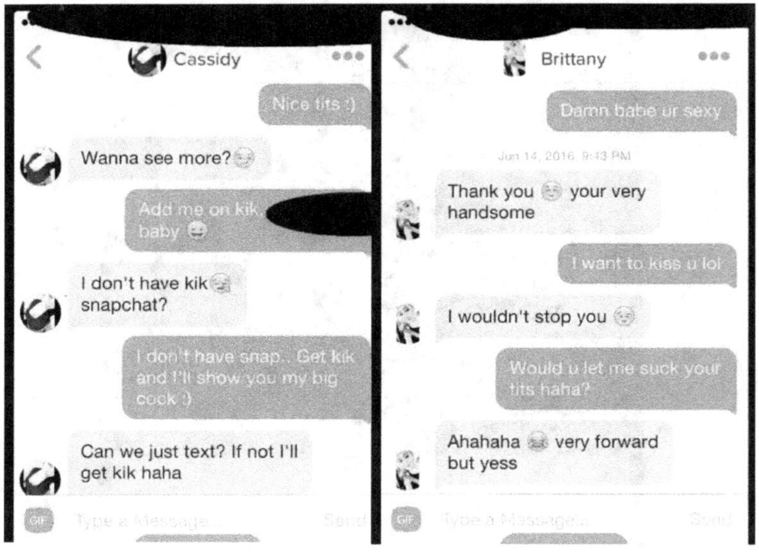


"Chadfishing" is parallel to catfishing since the core deceit is the same: luring unsuspecting people into virtual relationships under the pretense of intimacy.

Chadfishers are the more sadistic types of incels who have countless motives: revenge, loneliness, boredom, humiliation, attention, pleasure. Their overall goal is to prove that women will place physical appearance over any display of an awful personality.

If we are to believe the results of the various Chadfishing Tinder experimenting, females match with horrible rapists, white supremacists, and pedophiles and then carry-on conversations with these "fake" profiles.[4]

This evidence, if accurate, certainly does not provide a positive reflection of female sexuality but it does reveal how willing some might be to forego morality just to satisfy their innate desire. For the record, we would find comparable results in men.

And of course, single instances of personality not mattering (as we see in these experiments) does not conclusively debunk the notion that personality always matters or that it matters above everything else.

If one were to shrug off these experiments it would most likely be with the standard comeback, "it's just Tinder, which is a hook-up app – of course personality doesn't matter!" Even if this were true, it would still, entertainingly, prove that incels exist due to their below-average looks.

If incels were attractive, hooking-up would be more attainable and their basic need for human touch would be satisfied. It is worth recognizing, then, that the current dating app structure supports the notion that "personality does not matter." Because of this, incels are indefinitely excluded from participating – just for simply not being born attractive.

Is there a "looks do not matter" sexual intimacy app where photographs are excluded and you only swipe right or left based on someone's biography or character? *Of course not.* This speaks volumes about the importance of looks compared to that of personality.

It certainly needs to be recognized one more time – a looks only dating app exists, but a personality-only app does not. If personality is such a desirable trait, if not the most desired trait as is commonly claimed, why does an app with this type of feature not exist? We have dating apps for nearly every other niche, but not this one.

And all this begs the question: how much hooking up is actually happening via dating apps? If it is a lot, then incels are indeed missing out on an enormous piece of our shared human experience.

The position posited here, for clarity, is that the BOTH looks and personality compromise woman-to-man attraction and man-to-woman attraction. Both sexes prioritize looks over all other qualities. If casual sex is the goal, looks will be the most important consideration, of course. But at the same time looks will not drop in importance in more serious dating considerations.

## RESEARCH & CONCLUSION

There is now ample research on the impact and efficiency of communication technology on social relationships.[5] As such, it is hard to deny that smart phones have opened up and contributed to emerging dating markets and mating practices.

There are two primary benefits to smart phones — location based match-making and accessibility.

Smartphone technology makes dating available everywhere one goes.

In terms of popularity, one app stands out above the rest – Tinder. Whereas traditional web-based online models aimed to match users on interests, Tinder matches users primarily on attractiveness.

To be brief, again, Tinder provides the user base with potential nearby "matches" where they swipe right or swipe left to *like* or *dislike* other profiles. If both parties like each other, they are then given the opportunity to communicate via private messaging.

The internet is rife with articles describing frustration with online dating apps like Tinder. This is noteworthy considering these apps were intended to make dating easier and more efficient than ever.

One of the problems is that men and women tend to have very different approaches to online mating, a fact which often ends up producing frustration for both sides. Moreover, there is plenty of conversation about the "seriousness" of dating apps – whatever the case, Tinder is widely popular and has brought online mating to the masses.

It must be noted that, despite the widespread use of technological services, there is little extant research into Tinder or other matchmaking dating apps. However, motivations to use Tinder have recently been under scientific analysis; research has routinely established hooking-up as one of the primary motivators[6] and men were significantly more likely than women to use dating apps for casual sex partners.[7]

Conversely, one of the most comprehensive online dating studies[8] to date has determined that both genders are not simply using Tinder for hook-ups but to search for a partner for attention or just to chat. This fact is supported by the low rate at which people report meeting up with their matches, "73% of respondents estimated that 10% or fewer of their matches result in a real-world meet-up." This research was comprised of statistical data based on the research of about 230k male and 250k female profiles – so it was clearly exhaustive.

One of the more interesting findings of the study, in terms of evidence *against* the blackpill, is the following:

> "Without bios, our male stock profiles received an average of 16 matches from women; this increases four-fold to 69 with a bio."

This result suggests that women, in the majority of cases, are judging personality traits in some form. Perhaps it is because the men who lack a profile might be considered a one night stand?

Regardless, this further confirms that women do care about personality to some extent. But it does not disprove that they are picky about attractiveness, too.

In general, men tend to swipe right as much as possible in an attempt to get matches, while women on the contrary are far more selective.[9]

So, no matter how selective a woman might be when it comes to personality traits, some still have strict physical attributes from their must-haves list — recall the OkCupid study that which women rated a striking 80% of men less than medium attractiveness.

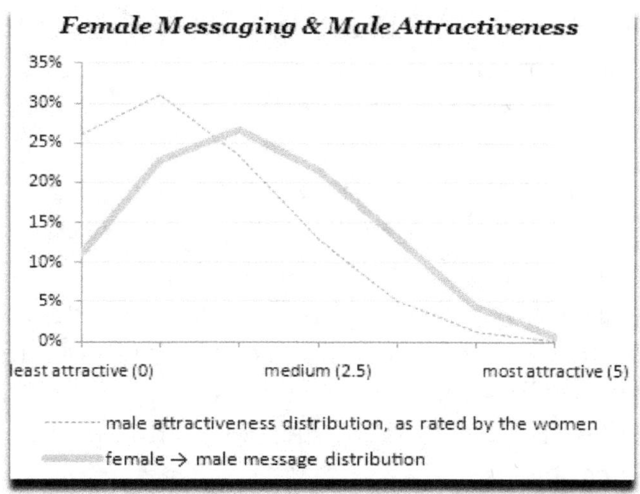



As noted by the dotted grey line, we can see the very harsh male attractiveness distribution as rated by women in the study.

And if we do accept that women are looking for love over casual sex on Tinder as research[10] has indicated – that is a pretty alarming implication, considering how brutally low women Tinder users rate men in terms of looks.

The depressing conclusion is that alongside the importance of personality evaluations, women *still* maintain high attractiveness standards, too.

Again, a quality character is valued but rarely detracts from the foundational demand for aesthetic beauty.

One could counter that Tinder, for example, has such a strong emphasis on physical appearances because there is only limited space for well-developed profiles. This would be a lazy argument, because Tinder allows the user to bring in outside social media to enhance one's profile. This includes both Instagram for social proof and Spotify for musical tastes.

Additionally, there was the enormous blackpill from the 2013 OkCupid, "Love is Blind," experiment[11]. OkCupid, undeniably has gone to the furthest lengths of any online dating product to match the users based on character traits and similarities in personality. On OkCupid, the user has the option to answer a wide variety of endless questions, take chemistry tests, and provide biographical information in order to potentially pair up with other like-minded individuals who have also provided their data.

Yet, when they conducted their experiment one conclusion was that "users were more likely to equate *looks* with *personality*, even in profiles that featured attractive photos and, little if any, substantive profile information."

Likewise, "when the site obscured all profile photos one day, users engaged in more meaningful conversations, exchanged more contact details and responded to first messages more often. They got to know each other. But when pictures were reintroduced on the site, many of those conversations stopped cold." Damn.

At this point, there will be a series of statements which will pave my way to the online dating conclusion. Each is logically consistent with the wide-ranging analysis above, and also with my own viewpoints, including the previous chapters on what women find attractive.

Everyone knows that dating apps have radically modified the dating paradigm in a way that it is taxing towards certain men. However, in my view this is not due to the fact that women are inherently only concerned with appearance. Bear with me here.

The reason it appears this way is because women call all or most of the shots over dating apps, and looks are the primary attribute for male success. But there is another explanation for this phenomenon than that women are fundamentally concerned with looks.

Remember that men are the selected sex and women are the selective sex. This does not mean men are inactive; on the contrary, men are in a constant state of competition to distinguish themselves in order to secure sex and reproduction.

In this experience, are women going around valuing the behavior of men and finding the worthiest to mate with? No – women start out inactive; the men come to them.

Although very few people will doubt the fact that women are largely inactive when it comes to online dating, many individuals like to venerate the position of women by suggesting that women mostly mate with men they find honorable, intelligent, kind, and so on.

Although unquestionably men with these traits often reproduce, the fundamental mistake lies here is the conflation of that which we intellectually appreciate and that which actually contributes to reproduction.

This phenomenon of simultaneously respecting certain behavior, while also engaging in contradictory behavior that tracks in order to gain reproductive success, is a duality exclusive to humans by virtue of our great intelligence.

It's helpful, when considering the vicissitudes of the sexual market to compare the relationships between men and women to a key and a lock. It is not that the lock is some discerning creature that repulses the keys that don't fit it; rather, it is by its nature a certain shape, and so only certain keys will be able to unlock it.

The onus is on the key to be the right shape; and what this means for men is to be the type of being that arouses the women's attraction. A woman can think what she wants about you, what she wants about herself, but ultimately biology cannot be escaped. If you hit the right combination of what attracts her, she will be yours.

What does this mean? Well, firstly, what attracts most women seems to be fairly consistent amongst all relevant personality research: the fittings of high status, power, dominance, competence, etc.

How does this relate to dating apps? Put simply, dating apps are disrupting the mating market because they constrain men from distinguishing themselves in any way besides physical attractiveness, because the power is completely in the women's hands.

Personality traits that arouse women cannot be communicated through a picture, and even if they could theoretically be communicated through texting, the only men that get to text women on dating apps are those who have been swiped right on (signifying the women approves of his appearance).

This reality has decimated the dating environment for unattractive men. Whether this disadvantages woman in a more remote way is an interesting question that will not be elaborated upon here.

Regardless, if this idea is reliable, it means that women are not shallow. It means that dating apps have steered their sexual dynamic into becoming shallow, because the only form by which a male can distinguish himself is physical attractiveness.

In this way, women only swipe right on attractive men because that is the only dimension of attractiveness that is expressed. Possibly, if women were more aware of what attracts them, they would be much more forgiving in appearance in order to allow themselves to see if the man's personality engages them?

With that said, the primitive nature of human sexuality is strong; it has been molded over a staggering period of time by evolution, and its implications are still largely unexplored.

In sum, desirable mental traits are basically the personality version of the halo-effect. Irrespective of the research focusing on online dating or just on general physical attractiveness[12], there *is* a looks threshold which acts as a gatekeeper for potential partners.

If a man meets a required level of physical attractiveness, then women are willing to consider his personality characteristics.

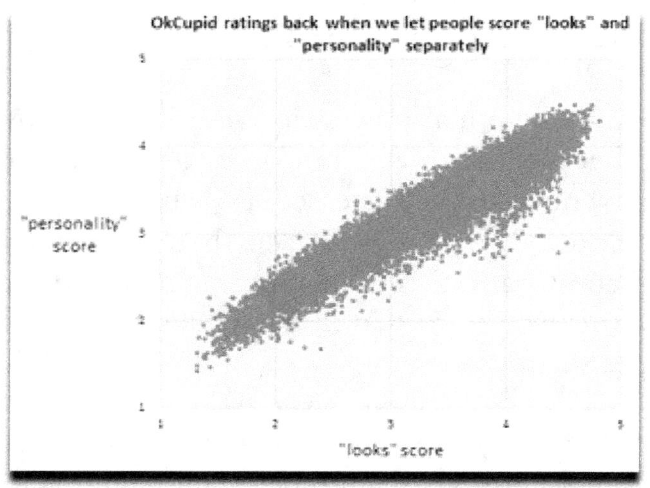


If a man does not meet the required level of physical attractiveness, then women tend to not give him a chance.

As such, people are wrong when they suggest dating is just about personality. It is more about how that personality is packaged.

Recall again the now deleted OkCupid "Love is Blind" experiment. The dot plot illustrates a direct correlation between a person's looks and their personality score.

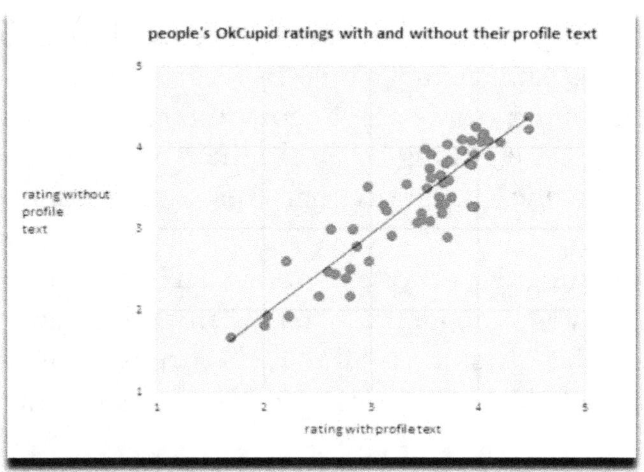


To confirm these initial findings indicating that most users only look at the profile pictures, OkCupid then displayed profile pictures with and without text and allowed users to rate.

In the words of OkCupid, "your picture is worth that fabled thousand words, but your actual words are worth…**almost nothing.**"

The question is, despite all the research, which is more important overall? It does not make sense to claim that one effect is much more overwhelmingly influential than the other.

Women evolved by carefully considering both physical and mental traits. Both attributes combat each other; they are deeply interwoven in the psyche, suggesting that women value physical attractiveness far more than they even recognize.

Unfortunately, on one hand, we have evidence out there which suggests a man's attractive face and muscular physique is all that she needs to override his horrible or even misogynistic character traits.

On the other hand, it is uncertain whether or not a great, witty biography can override equally unfortunate deficiencies in physical appearance.

I favor avoiding anecdotal evidence as much as possible but I know some pretty well-rounded, great guys who *never* match with women. Never.

For men, these technologies have separated users into two distinct leagues: the haves and the have nots.

The bourgeoisie and the proletariat. An elite class of men have most of the success with online dating. Study after study confirms this.

Recall the original online dating blackpill premise: relationship choices are made after a total assessment of features. Assuming all features are weighted equally, it would be entirely unreasonable to blame dating app failures on just a single feature, like looks.

In other words, personality does play a part in online dating success. So, if a man is struggling to acquire both matches and dates, we can blame their failures on both physical and mental attributes.

The only exception here would be the men rated the highest of the genetically elite, the gentlemen that incels refer to as the "Chad's" — they can pretty much get away with any type of conversation and still be successful.

With this noted, my premise presumes that there is a threshold for both attractiveness *and* personality.

This position, based on all the research that we have, is logically consistent with the blackpill.

To be a successful online dater, at least for a man, he needs to be above some arbitrary attractiveness level.

For simplicity, let us assume that if a man is a below a 3/10 on an attractiveness rating scale, he will receive zero matches. As such, an incel who falls below this 3/10 threshold and therefore blames his physical flaws on his lack of online dating success is correct. This incel may or may not also have personality and social flaws, but he is absolutely correct when he recognizes his height and facial aesthetics are holding him back, as well.

Even after all the evidence presented above, there will still be some who will continue denying that being unattractive is what is holding the incel back. They will stick to their guns and place the entire blame on his personality. Why isn't this suggestion just as absurd as suggesting that personality does not matter whatsoever when it comes to relationships?

Appearances play a significant role in how we feel emotionally about something or someone. Feeling deeply attracted to another person fulfills a profound psychological need. As such, whether the discussion is something casual or something more serious, looks are indispensable.

The logical conclusion is this: try to avoid online dating or hookup apps. That would be a great idea, were it not for the fact that the alternatives are rapidly dwindling and online dating is becoming increasingly popular, the standard for dating as a whole.

And if dating moves entirely online, then women will select for looks primarily, given that it is nearly impossible to get a sense of a man's personality through a dating profile.

# VII. WHAT CAN YOU DO IF YOU'RE AN INCEL

Incels read this book and now all the pain manifests, and it hurts. It hurts to know that they are not in control. It hurts to know they have implicit biases just like everyone else.

Even "normies" realize that they may have, at some point, played a part in causing some emotional pain towards incels. That is why their reactions are to lump all of them into one idea of "toxicity," just to protect themselves from their own pain.

Incels are not crazy, although some of them certainly do take it too far and hold extreme, damaging ideas. From what I have observed, I believe that the majority of incels are self-aware enough to understand extremism when they see it. That said, anger and frustration leads to venting, and I hate seeing people taking everything being said online as genuine misogynistic plans and opinions.

I do believe many incels swallow the blackpill and then just dwell on it. They spend all their time Chadfishing and making themselves miserable. It's masochistic. But it does not need to be like this.

As was stated in the beginning, the blackpill transcends beyond dating prospects as it provides an understanding of our existence as a whole. The blackpill is acceptance of the world as it is WITHOUT morality.

Men and women are part of nature, and their actions emerge from their survival instincts. Just as we cannot be upset at wolves for hunting sheep, being upset at women because she did not reciprocate one's romantic or sexual desires is wasted energy.

Nature is amoral, not good or evil. Again, is the lion evil for murdering buffalo or zebra? Of course not.

If you believe in the blackpill the only conclusion you can come to is that it is not women's fault. This is how it is and how it has always been. This is nature.

Women were effectively required for a millennium, due to enforced monogamy, to stay with unattractive men just because they were not allowed realistic opportunities otherwise. Now that women are able to have careers, live on their own, and provide for themselves, they can be more selective when it comes to physical preferences.

*It is society which is completely at fault for lying, not women.* This realization does not always make it easier but it is a harsh reality, that needs to be accepted. Considering this, I am not suggesting to view life as meaningless after developing a blackpilled awareness. Instead, I would suggest that life be viewed as a struggle. The parameters should be recognized, and individuals should work hard to find creative ways to overcome their personal roadblocks.

Flattening the dating preferences between the sexes is not a winnable cope to cling onto. The current status quo is not going to change. Society is powerless to stop this and that is why they have been lying to you for so long. Of course, it is not easy to undo faulty societal conditioning, but it's not impossible, either.

Most people who accept the blackpill are probably people with higher than average IQ. Because to become blackpilled takes a certain level of self-awareness, introspection, and ability to recognize patterns. Notice how a dog has zero self-awareness – he will just walk outside and take a shit regardless of who is watching. That is because the less intelligent have less self-awareness.

For the incels with a blackpilled awareness, the truth is acknowledged intellectually but their bodies still won't allow them to accept that they are not a part of the mating market. These biological urges create a desperation to breed that bring them continued despair, and in some cases, ruin their lives. The body does not give a fuck – it will push you to do all you can to reproduce – even if you have determined in your mind that this is hopeless.

## SELF-IMPROVEMENT & A POSITIVE MINDSET

A lot of people make personal growth way too complicated when it really does not need to be. Gobs of bluepilled self-improvement literature already exists out there.  Most of it is an absolute waste of time.

As an incel, you are most likely here because you are physically unattractive, so the focus of this section is to offer 5 simple, but effective methods to improve your overall mental and physical self.

- Lift weights. Go to the gym. Exercise. Run. Learn how to box. All these help with depression. Plus, most women prefer a fit guy over a flabby guy. Even aside from sexual interest or a better body, it portrays dedication and drive, which are attractive. Please keep in mind that one cannot "out-science" bad genetics with following a strict and flawless scientific based lifting regimen. There are limits to what is achievable without the use of synthetic hormones.

- Put the fork down.  We have an obesity epidemic. If you are overweight: lose weight. It will not only help your bodily appearance — it will also work wonders towards facial attractiveness.

- Get a hobby. Preferably one which gets you outside and moving. Moderates amounts of sun are good for the body. Plus, this will give you an opportunity to meet and socialize with people of both sexes. Hiking is great for this; joining a running club is, too. Dance classes are also good.

- Work on your "inner-game." I know this one sounds like absolute bulshit but it is important. Try to improve your mindset a little every single day. Meditate. Do yoga. Once you begin to understand that the way we are perceived by others is out of our control, it will only make perfect sense to develop a solid relationship with yourself.

- Plastic surgery. We need to remove the stigma surrounding plastic surgery, especially for men, and stop lying to them that their looks do not matter. If you are an incel because of being born with a weak, receding jaw, surgery is really the only solution. This can be surgically corrected and it can potentially fix the problem for good. Of course, plastic surgery is not exactly inexpensive, so it will not be accessible to all incels.

As the two graphics[1] indicate, just a few millimeters of bone movement are more than enough to turn an unattractive incel into handsome man.

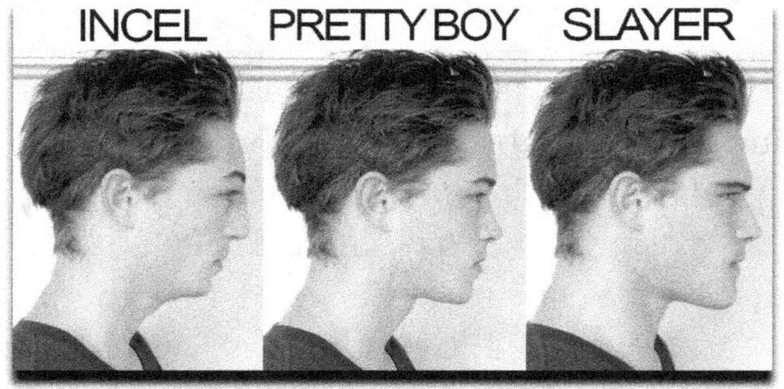


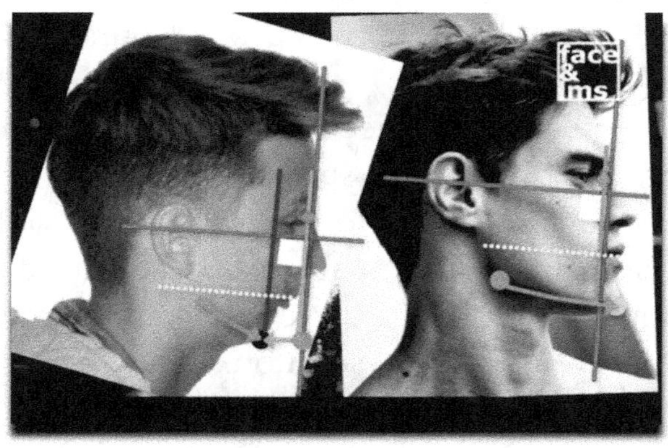


Many incels have room to improve, whether they want to admit it or not. Some have poor habits, they know what they are, and how they can be overcome. Of course, how those are handled is up to the individual. He needs to assess his own what the problems and develop his own plan for solving them.

---

## Is Therapy Worth It?

---

Perhaps Freud said it best: the objective of therapy is to turn unbearable suffering into normal everyday miserability.[2]

Therapy is very useful when the problem is in your head. However, if you are physically ugly, and treated like an outcast and you feel like shit because of this, there is little a therapist can do for you. This is external suffering.

The whole premise of therapy is that if you change the way you think about a real problem, somehow you change the problem. This is false.

Therapy will not cure inceldom, it will not make the face better, or the limbs longer. As was uncovered repeatedly, men are largely valued on their physical characteristics. The bigger, stronger, and better looking one is, the more he is valued and respected, by women and men alike.

If the incel is getting ignored or ridiculed at work or by the opposite sex, these are real feelings. They are not "in his head."

A physically disabled person, for example, might have issues resulting from their external conditions which leads to depression. It is a logical and rational thing. Not being able to find work because of the disability could also be depressing. Again, this is an external issue developing into an internal issue. You can draw a straight line from one to the other.

The problem is, it seems psychotherapists do not know how to deal with inceldom. There are remarkably few articles about this significant and pervasive problem. This, too, may change if the society gave sincere attention to this situation.

I genuinely believe that a quality, open-minded therapist could guide an incel towards a better life. But if the client is unattractive and short, as we need to recognize that most incels are, that is a tough one. What is the strategy?

Inceldom therapy requires education, recommendations, and suggestions which are not typically covered in conventional therapy. Also, the public backlash for this type of therapy could be devastating in itself, especially when claims of misogyny or something alike could easily be declared.

With that acknowledged, if someone is treated terribly (for any reason), therapy can help build emotional resilience so that the mistreatment and traumas are at least not as damaging.

On the point of ugliness, obviously, therapy cannot change one's physiology. But therapy can improve the way an incel views himself. Of course, it will not make a 3/10 see himself as a 9/10, but therapy might at least stop him from feeling like a 1. It might give him tools to work with what he has.

There's a very fine line between encouraging people to work on the things they have control over, and victim blaming them for their circumstances. There's nothing wrong with the former, indeed it may even help somewhat. But ultimately, there are no personal solutions to systemic problems.

With that said, there are examples of former incels who have turned their lives around for the better. They determined that the pain of staying the same was greater than the pain of changing. So, they changed. Others have chosen to reject animal nature and live his life on artificial pleasures (escapism). For some, this even involves rejecting their sexuality wholesale.

---

## MGTOW

---

"MGTOW" stands for Men Going Their Own Way. The three main principles are simply:

1. No cohabitating.
2. No marriage.
3. No children.

MGTOW is not about hating women. It is merely walking away from the current sexual marketplace because of the real or perceived flaws inherent in getting into relationships, having children, or getting married.

For clarity, MGTOW is not a *movement*; it is an individual lifestyle choice.

Feminism is a movement. Gay pride is a movement. They rely heavily on arranged public events conceived to draw attention to the cause and common goals. MGTOW is the opposite of that.

With that noted, MGTOW is not just about living a life without cohabitation. It can also be an enlightenment process to learn and discover more truths about oneself and the world.

MGTOW is a blackpill idea because the general sentiment that fighting for men's rights is totally pointless because nobody cares. So, MGTOW says, men might as well just drop out entirely and "go their own way."

The common mantra across MGTOW forums are to avoid the illusion of "happy wife, happy life" which society has sold to them. As such, this type of conviction can certainly be very appealing to an incel who has never had a relationship in the first place.

The danger of the "happy wife" fantasy, according to MGTOW, is that it might lead to choices that are objectively harmful, based on the illusion of reality. For example, humans still get married despite knowing that ~50% of marriages end in divorce, and that divorce is a costly endeavor.

Then after finalizing their divorce and giving away half their resources, many proceed to get married again, and again, inviting constant personal and financial turmoil. Such marriage decisions take place when one approaches them with a warped view of reality.

An incel considering going his own way will need to come to the realization that his original programming, both as a product of biology and society, can be undone but only if the right questions are asked.

Instead of asking "How do I find a woman?" ask, "Why should I find a woman?" Or instead of asking, "When will I ever get a girlfriend?" ask, "Why should I want a girlfriend?"

MGTOWs claim men have started off with faulty premises from the very beginning which have led to faulty conclusions.

If we start with the premise that "we need a girlfriend to be happy," then it logically follows that we will look for solutions that include how to get one. Keep asking "why" rather than settling for the initial conclusions. Instead of fantasizing about a future with a nuclear family, try and plan for other things.

MGTOWs, in general, are men who believe happiness does not need to be found in other people. If you adhere to finding happiness in others, then you will be disappointed eventually.

There are several benefits to MGTOW. A single man has time to pursue a variety of hobbies, quit his job whenever, vacation whenever or wherever desired, live minimalistically, save more money, work less, and retire earlier, among other benefits. Life is undoubtedly much easier and less expensive if the conclusion is to "go your own way."

Although MGTOW can be a viable outlet for some incels, there are obviously unfortunate societal ramifications attached to the idea.

Beyond that, many incels are not interested in MGTOW. They want a wife. They want families. They want love. They want romance. But the current trends suggest that inceldom will continue to rise — it's still only in its infancy — so this will never be a realistic possibility for millions of men being left behind.

As such, MGTOW might be the only option.

## CONSEQUENCES OF INCELDOM ON SOCIETY

I do believe one of the primary reasons we have not seen any significant solution offered to these lonely young men — besides shaming tactics or sex robots — is because that we do not have any effective means of helping them.

It appears the current choice is to sweep inceldom issues under the rug, because they lead to uncomfortable conversations. Scientists cannot even look into these problems because funding what's been labelled as "misogynistic" research is problematical. All of this reinforces our taboos.

Our society is built upon inequality and even discrimination. Even openly so. Think about the homeless, or the disabled, unattractive people. All these groups are invisible according to the media — they do not appear on television or film. Even in our everyday lives, there are few disabled CEOs, or unattractive managers, individuals with disabilities of any kind in positions of power.

The problem is that no one is discussing these issues and the factors contributing to them. And there has never been a meaningful campaign, no institution for spreading awareness, and no honest media representation.

These problems cannot be rectified if they are left in the darkness. We cannot have a real discourse about them they are relegated to the shadows. But there *does* need to be a concerted effort to tackle the situation and combat the media. I do believe the media is a large part of the problem, especially with the perpetuation of stereotypes by association in nearly every article.

This begins and ends with the current dating environment. In today's mating market, dating is increasingly unequal, reinforcing loneliness and contributing to the overall segregation of millions of people.

The dating participants, both men and women, in the market are expected to possess a limitless number of attributes if they want to be perceived as worthy by other participants.

The attributes vary according to gender, but according to all relevant research, presently it is men who do not only need to possess a longer required list of attributes but also, each of them, far more challenging to attain than the attributes that they desire in women.

For example, if a woman is expected to be young and physically attractive a man is expected to be "economically attractive," physically attractive, over six feet tall, intelligent, funny, well-educated, with a full head of hair, and a vibrant social life. The list of countless requirements men are expected to have is simply unrealistic for the vast majority of them.

If, in addition to lack of economic opportunities, genetical factors such as looks are depriving men from high paying jobs – with the understanding now that rewards, advancements, and better opportunities are being given to men who possess better physical attributes – then the current dating market will continue to exclude millions of men.

This means that the mating market has become a producer of recognizable social inequalities, since the great majority of men, no matter the effort made, are being left behind with little or no prospects for finding partners. While a few select men – without any significant effort – have no problem finding multiple dating partners.

"Don't be an incel!" "Get rich!" "Hit the gym, you are not tall enough!" And "beautiful queens only deserve handsome men" clichés only reinforce the narrative that the current mating market is unfair, biased, and contributes to the social rejection of millions.

This observation, naturally, is considered as irrelevant and even as a positive feature by those participants in the current dating market, who are benefitting from reduced competition due to the large majority of men being totally excluded from realistic dating aspirations.

Even if one does ascend and find a partner, irrespective of being a man or a woman, they can still opt out of the relationship and enter into a new partnership with just one swipe, in little to no time.

This leads to the conclusion that not only does the current unregulated mating market have lopsided upstream possibilities for participants but also leads to unfairness in downstream results.

Our society used to enforce and encourage monogamy, stable marriages, and the nuclear family until very recently. Now, in terms of relationship patterns, we are gradually reverting to *something* else, something that revolves more around the paradigm of swiping apps.

If there lies a fault to this societal change, whose fault, is it?

The incels will blame women proclaiming that it is their fault for not finding them attractive. The rest of the world will proclaim it is incel's fault for being bitter and entitled. Both are wrong.

The accountability lies partially with the cultural shifts which began about 50 years ago, which brought many positives to society, but certainly began the decline of the nuclear family model, in general, and romantic satisfaction, in particular.

The other part of the accountability, lies squarely behind the makeovers in just in the last decades marked keenly by the rise of social media and introduction of dating apps into the mating market. As a result, we are observing, in both sexes:

- Shorter term relationships and the rise of individualism.
- Unspoken sexual exclusivity, while keeping all options open, during the search for optimal partners.
- Marital rates declining and showing zero sign of slowing.
- A steady increase in the number of sexless men as a whole, especially those men at the bottom of the mating hierarchy.

- An imbalance of persons who have access to a willing mate for sex and/or intimacy – and those that do not. For women, this is practically always a choice, as they are gatekeepers of sex, for men this is increasingly involuntary.[3]
- The blossoming of non-monogamist identities and expressions.

Ultimately, as in a number's game, if the majority feels that the mating game is rigged against them and no matter the degree of efforts they decide to put in, the rigging will not disappear. On the contrary, it may worsen, and these millions of rejected men – whose aspirations are being denied by a society who sees them as completely worthless for not possessing the "required" attributes – know that the only way for them to achieve satisfactory outcomes is through a substantial change of the current mating market. Which is just not going to happen.

As I see it, society is never going to have an immediate and effective public regulation that reintroduces "fairness" into the unequal mating market.

As such, society will continue to ignore the needs and prospects millions of incels are currently failing to meet, not viewing their unmet aspirations as relevant enough. As a consequence, the millions of excluded and discriminated will not have any option left but to opt out of a system that disregards them.

With the current disconsideration of the critical thinking and rhetoric necessary to discuss inceldom, especially in the United States, men will continue to check out economically. Some will also check out entirely, via suicide.

Of course, the exact causes of suicide cannot be agreed upon as the findings are all over the place, and the explanations transcend beyond explanations of the economy and romantic satisfaction. Nevertheless, heavy technology and social media usage have also both been associated with poor mental health[4].

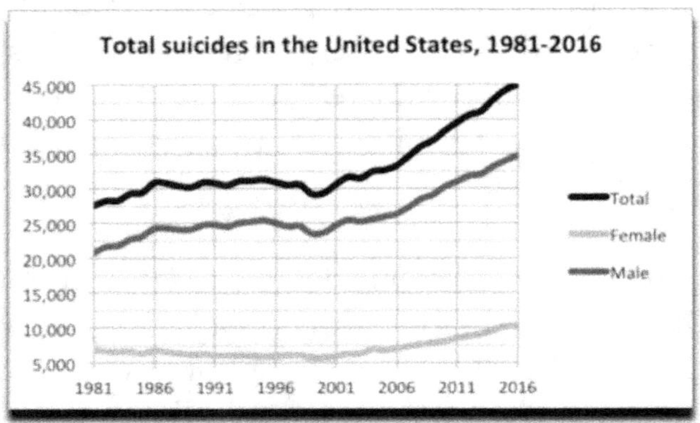


Regardless, let's stop evading the elephant in the room: if our society wants to continue pretending the inceldom does not exist for the sake of convenience, and remain oblivious to the suffering and hardships endured by millions of excluded men, the fallout will be inevitable.

Inceldom *is* a ticking time bomb, but not because of a future sexless male cataclysm against civilization. No.

It is a ticking bomb because our current society functions as long as men operate under the illusion that they can advance their lot in life through hard work and social conformity. Once that illusion breaks, men will become either destructive or lazy, and either one of those would result in drastic societal changes.

I do understand and recognize that what I have said here can come off as exaggerated or extreme, but all I have stated can be easily observed. I am also well aware that there have been destructive acts committed by men (incels and non-incels). Unmistakably, that is not something anyone would encourage, but it is somewhat shocking it does not happen more often, all things considered.

Recently, mainstream media has even started publishing pieces about these observations. If you have ever read an article about – the "drop in sex," the "marriage decline," or the "baby drought" – you have probably noted that the reflections within the articles are similar. But the conclusions to explain the phenomena are all wrong.

Modern thinkers cannot agree on much, but it is almost universally agreed upon that nature is not always good. This applies to human nature as well, and in this case specifically the way that men and women are programmed to browse the DNA pool, so to speak.

For those readers who have made it this far, the blackpill necessitates a lot of mental strength, because just knowing about it takes a certain responsibility from then on.

The bluepill Disney dream life of the white picket fence and a loving family was definitely a much simpler and in many ways more fulfilling fantasy. But it was just that: a *fantasy*. Remember, the blackpill is the realization of what is really going on. Even though it can be saddening, there still *can* be positive outcomes to all of this.

After internalizing that looks are of paramount importance and personality is secondary, at best, one should become noticeably less socially anxious.

Moreover, after knowing this truth, one should feel liberated, be less sexist, more understanding of women's behavior, more conscious about the struggles of others, more realistic about one's potential achievements, more thankful for what one has, less likely to treat someone differently because of their physical appearance, less confused about why some men succeed with dating while others do not, and less frustrated overall.

The blackpill is also a far superior mode of living than the bluepill. A bluepilled man will spend his entire life hating himself for everything out of his personal control. A blackpilled man no longer needs to blame himself when he gets gaslighted by platitudes such as, "just be confident," "make her laugh," "be a good listener," etc. He will understand and accept that women are rejecting any advances for traits largely because of his genes, his looks.

Living a life where you blame yourself for all of your romantic shortcomings is horrible. Believing one has a terrible personality, is not sociable enough, and lacks confidence can be lot more mentally damaging than accepting the truth of the blackpill.

Under this approach to life, it is no longer necessary to spend years worrying about attracting women and being scared of not having romantic success. There is nothing morally wrong with being an unattractive man. Being constantly rejected and forever single is not a personal failing.

The blackpill allows one to realize that all paths, for the most part, are already determined by bone.

What you are is what you are.

______________________________

# Notes

## INTRODUCTION

[1] Body image dissatisfaction refers to a person's negative perception of his or her own physical appearance. Body image is defined as "the concern with internal, subjective representations of physical appearance and bodily experience."
Cash, T. F., & Pruzinsky, T. E. (1990). Body images: Development, deviance, and change. Guilford Press.
-Body image contains emotional (e.g., feelings and affect), cognitive (e.g., evaluation), behavioral (e.g., positive and negative health behaviors), and perceptual (e.g., awareness of body size) components.
McCabe, M. P., & Ricciardelli, L. A. (2004). Body image dissatisfaction among males across the lifespan: A review of past literature. Journal of psychosomatic research, 56(6), 675-685.
-Masculinities studies is broadly concerned with the societal construction of what it means to "be a man." According to Michael Kimmel, "masculinity" refers to the behaviors and social roles

within a given society as well as the symbolic meanings attributed to them.
Kimmel, M. S., & Davis, T. (2011). Mapping guyland in college. In Masculinities in higher education (pp. 19-31). Routledge.

[2] A netnography is qualitative, interpretive methodological research approach that adapts the traditional, in-person ethnographic research techniques to study online communities. Virtual communities are an increasingly significant channel for people to share their feelings and experiences regarding specific issues. As part of the analysis of this book, I aimed to reveal the experiences and feelings of involuntary celibate men, in order to better understand the nature of the community. I analyzed thousands and thousands of threads and posts from self-described incel subscribers, primarily from the website reddit.com. The specific reddit communities were r/incels (until it was banned from reddit on November 7, 2017) and then r/braincels which became the most popular subreddit to discuss community issues after the banning of r/incels. Upon the completion of this book r/braincels was banned by reddit on September 30, 2019).

[3] Nearly half of all college students have clinical depression as 41% moderate to severe depression is more than a bit bothersome. And according to the National Institute of Mental Health (NIMH) it is not just United States college students, suicidal ideation has been skyrocketing with pre-teens as well. (Lanzillo, E.C., Horowitz, L.M., Wharff, E.A., Sheftall, A.H., Pao, M., & Bridge, J.A. (in press). The importance of screening preteens for suicide risk in the emergency department. Hospital Pediatrics).

## CHAPTER I

---

[4] This information is sourced from the latest data from the General Social Survey. The two graphs are from the Washington Post. https://www.washingtonpost.com/business/2019/03/29/share-americans-not-having-sex-has-reached-record-high/ (last accessed: 07.21.2019)

[5] In Japan, young men are abstaining from sex in record highs and the population is decreasing at alarming rates. These Japanese men have been given the label "herbivores." While the goal of this book is to not make future prognostications, the sexual culture of the West seems to be on a similar trajectory, even though the Japanese have different reasons for their incelibacy crisis.

[6] The term "incel" was actually first coined by a woman named Alana, in 1997. She started a website, Alana's Involuntary Celibacy Project, which was for lonely people struggling to find love.

[7] Normies are perfectly 'normal' everyday people who believe everything they are told without question and refuse to see the 'truth' about whatever the subject in question is, they believe in the system and would give their lives to it. In other words, a "normie" is the regular-ass boring person; one with standard held mainstream beliefs, ideas, or interests. A normie goes to college, finds a girlfriend, gets married, buys a house in some bland subdivision, has two children, leases a mini-van, then gets divorced seven years later. The basic life script – this is what you are "supposed" to do – to be accepted as a "normal" person in society.

[8] Van Straaten, I., Engels, R. C., Finkenauer, C., & Holland, R. W. (2009). Meeting your match: How attractiveness similarity affects approach behavior in mixed-sex dyads. *Personality and Social Psychology Bulletin, 35*(6), 685-697.

[9] Graphs are archived here: https://web.archive.org/web/20171128111858/https://theblog.o

kcupid.com/your-looks-and-your-inbox-8715c0f1561e                    (last accessed 09.12.2019)
I do not believe any information has been disclosed to explain why the OkCupid studies are now memory holed, but it would make financial sense to remove discouraging data. With that said, the previous head of data analytics at OkCupid, Christian Rudder, has a book called "Dataclysm" – that is where these graphs originate from; he goes into the methodology which was all done very carefully with data sets of unprecedented sizes; it is more or less the largest scale analysis of human behavior we have available on modern dating apps. Again, this OkCupid research has been deleted from the internet but it is discussed in greater detail in the "Dating Apps" section.

[10]Neyt, Vanderbulcke, Baert (2019). "Are men intimidated by highly educated women? Undercover on Tinder." Economics of Education Review, 73, 101914.

[11] Kopf, D. (2017). "These statistics show why it's so hard to be an average man on dating apps." https://qz.com/1051462/these-statistics-show-why-its-so-hard-to-be-an-average-man-on-dating-apps/ (last accessed 10.01.2019).

[12] Robert, T. (1972). Parental investment and sexual selection. Sexual Selection & the Descent of Man, Aldine de Gruyter, New York, 136-179.

[13] Regnerus, M. (2017). *Cheap sex: The transformation of men, marriage, and monogamy*. Oxford University Press.

[14] Kontula, O., & Haavio-Mannila, E. (2003). Masturbation in a generational perspective. Journal of Psychology & Human Sexuality, 14(2-3), 49-83.

[15] Statistics from Toronto's Redpath Centre as found on

https://www.theglobeandmail.com/life/relationships/single-with-autism-its-complicated/article14797656/ (last accessed 09.01.2019)

[16] Schöttle and colleagues (2017). Sexuality in autism. hypersexual and paraphilic behavior in women and men with high-functioning autism spectrum disorder. Dialogues Clin Neurosci; 19 (4): 381

[17] Chart and data found here: https://incels.co/threads/survey-results-for-october-2019.147774/#lg=_xfUid-1-1573141713&slide=0  (last accessed: 11.01.2019)

[18] The poll was open to anyone who identifies as an incel and who was r/braincels community member. This thread (and the entire r/braincels forum) has since been deleted by reddit.com by the time of publishing this book. This is the old URL, where the poll was administered, it is no longer accessible.
https://www.reddit.com/r/Braincels/comments/ai6g3o/braincels_raceage_poll_results/

[19] US Census Information updated 2018.
https://www.census.gov/quickfacts/fact/table/US/PST045218

[20] All survey results from October 2019 poll, conducted on incels.co, can be accessed here: https://incels.co/threads/survey-results-for-october-2019.147774/ (last accessed 10.29.2019)

[21] Jaki, S., De Smedt, T., Gwóźdź, M., Panchal, R., Rossa, A., & De Pauw, G. (2018). Online hatred of women in the Incels. me forum: Linguistic analysis and automatic detection. Manuscript submitted.
https://organisms.be/downloads/incels.pdf (last accessed: 11.01.2019).

[22] Himes, D. (2018). "Men's declining labor force participation"
https://www.bls.gov/opub/mlr/2018/beyond-bls/mens-declining-labor-force-participation.htm (last assessed 09.12.2019).

---

[23] In its simplest definition, a collapsitarianism believes society is on the way to collapse. In a general sense, it is a belief that the "system" will slowly degenerate as a process and a worthier system will take it over. This mantra has become more popular across the manosphere, it is just not an exclusive incel belief.

[24] As of 09.15.2019 the screenshotted tweet is still publicly available at https://twitter.com/ekp/status/991817194987114496

[25] Ellis, L., & Walsh, A. (2000). Criminology: A global perspective. Allyn and Bacon.

[26] Palmer, C. T., & Tilley, C. F. (1995). Sexual access to females as a motivation for joining gangs: An evolutionary approach. Journal of Sex Research, 32(3), 213-217.


## CHAPTER II

[1] Westfall, R. S., Millar, M. G., & Lovitt, A. (2019). The Influence of physical attractiveness on belief in a just world. Psychological reports, 122(2), 536-549.

[2] The fundamental attribution error is the tendency for people to over-emphasize dispositional, or personality-based explanations for behaviors observed in others while under-emphasizing situational explanations. In other words, people have a cognitive bias to assume that a person's actions depend on what "type" of person that person is rather than on the environmental forces that influence the person.


## CHAPTER III

[1] Rudder, C. (2014). "Dataclysm: Love, Sex, Race, and Identity--What Our Online Lives Tell Us about Our Offline Selves." Crown.

[2] Prum, R. O. (2017). The evolution of beauty: How Darwin's forgotten theory of mate choice shapes the animal world-and us. Anchor.

[3] The 'positive feedback loop' consists in one sex evolving to be more attracted to a particular feature in the other sex for the mere reason that it is selected by others, but as the population overall evolves stronger attraction to the feature, the evolutionary pressure grows exponentially to be even more attracted to the feature. This results in exaggeration or over-complication of said feature in the other sex in efforts to evolve to become more attractive.

[4] The 'attractiveness halo effect' is where desired personality traits are ascribed to attractive people over unattractive people. For example, the influence of one's appearance can be used as a cue when attempting to accurately perceive health or intelligence (Dion, Bersheid, & Walster, 1972). https://www.ncbi.nlm.nih.gov/pubmed/4655540/

[5] PUA stands for "pick-up artist." It implies a lot of things, but today it mostly represents a douchebag who attempts to hit on several women in hopes that one will have sex with him. In other words, the PUA movement of the era was mostly an obnoxious group of straight men who practiced the art of approaching straight women with the intention of quickly building attraction and sexual escalation.

**CHAPTER IV**

[1] Hamermesh, D. S., and J. E. Biddle (1994): "Beauty and the Labor Market," The American Economic Review, 84(5), 1174–1194.

[2] Mobius, M. M., & Rosenblat, T. S. (2006). Why beauty matters. American Economic Review, 96(1), 222-235.

[3] Feingold, A. (1992). Good-looking people are not what we think. Psychological bulletin, 111(2), 304.

[4] Langlois, J. H., Kalakanis, L., Rubenstein, A. J., Larson, A., Hallam, M., & Smoot, M. (2000). Maxims or myths of beauty? A meta-analytic and theoretical review. Psychological bulletin, 126(3), 390.

[5] Dion, K., Berscheid, E., & Walster, E. (1972). What is beautiful is good. Journal of Personality and Social Psychology, 24(3), 285–290. doi:10.1037/h0033731

[6] Minerva, F. (2017). The Invisible Discrimination Before Our Eyes: A Bioethical Analysis. Bioethics, 31(3), 180-189.

[7] Benzeval, M., Green, M. J., & Macintyre, S. (2013). Does perceived physical attractiveness in adolescence predict better socioeconomic position in adulthood? Evidence from 20 years of follow up in a population cohort study. PloS one, 8(5), e63975.

[8] Bertrand, M., & Mullainathan, S. (2004). Are Emily and Greg more employable than Lakisha and Jamal? A field experiment on labor market discrimination. American economic review, *94*(4), 991-1013.

[9] Quinn, P. C., Kelly, D. J., Lee, K., Pascalis, O., & Slater, A. M. (2008). Preference for attractive faces in human infants extends beyond conspecifics. Developmental science, 11(1), 76-83.

[10] Eleftheriou, A., Bullock, S., Graham, C. A., Stone, N., & Ingham, R. (2016). Does attractiveness influence condom use intentions in heterosexual men? An experimental study. BMJ open, 6(6), e010883.

[11] Sela, Y., Weekes-Shackelford, V. A., Shackelford, T. K., & Pham, M. N. (2015). Female copulatory orgasm and male partner's attractiveness to his partner and other women. Personality and Individual Differences, 79, 152-156.

[12] Puts, D. A., Welling, L. L., Burriss, R. P., & Dawood, K. (2012). Men's masculinity and attractiveness predict their female partners' reported orgasm frequency and timing. Evolution and Human Behavior, 33(1), 1-9.

[13] The Pareto Principle (or the 80/20 rule) is named after Italian economist Vifredo Pareto's observation that 80% of the land in Italy was by 20% of the population. It terms of sexual dynamics, the pareto principle suggests that 20% of men are consuming 80% of the sex. In other words, according to this idea, a man needs to be in the top 20% of all men (physically, professionally) to have any sexual relationship with a woman.

[14] Neyt, B., Vandenbulcke, S., & Baert, S. (2019). Are men intimidated by highly educated women? Undercover on Tinder. *Economics of Education Review, 73*, 101914.

[15] See section, Dual Mating Strategy & Hypergamy

[16] Anderson, R. M. (2013). Positive sexuality and its impact on overall well-being. Bundesgesundheitsblatt – Gesundheitsforschung - Gesundheitsschutz, 56(2), 208-214.

[17] Flynn, T. J., & Gow, A. J. (2015). Examining associations between sexual behaviours and quality of life in older adults. Age and ageing, 44(5), 823-828.

[18] Loprinzi, P. D., & Nooe, A. (2015). Erectile dysfunction and mortality in a national prospective cohort study. The journal of sexual medicine, 12(11), 2130-2133.

---

[19] Image borrowed from https://www.simplypsychology.org/maslow.html (last accessed: 03.10.2019)

[20] Maslow's Hierarchy of Needs is more of a conceptual model that is useful for illustration, than a verified science. It still offers a both a practical understanding of motivation and a necessary humanistic aspect to psychology.

[21] Tanner, J. (2019). Human development https://www.britannica.com/science/human-development/Development-of-the-reproductive-organs-and-secondary-sex-characteristics (last accessed: 10.11.2019)

[22] Graph and data borrowed from https://incels.co/threads/survey-results-for-october-2019.147774/ (last accessed: 11.01.2019)

[23] Cigna. (2018). Research Puts Spotlight on the Impact of Loneliness in the U.S. and Potential Root Causes https://www.cigna.com/newsroom/news-releases/2018/new-cigna-study-reveals-loneliness-at-epidemic-levels-in-america (last assessed: 04.21.2019)

[24] James BD, Wilson RS, Barnes LL, Bennett DA. (2011). Late-life social activity and cognitive decline in old age. Journal of the International Neuropsychological Society 17 (6) pp. 998-1005.

[25] Holt-Lunstad J, TB, Layton JB. (2010). Social relationships and mortality risk: a meta-analytic review. *PLoS Medicine* 7 (7)
Hawkley LC, Thisted RA, Masi CM, Cacioppo JT. (2010). Loneliness predicts increased blood pressure: 5-year cross-lagged analyses in middle-aged and older adults. Psychology and Aging 25 (1) pp.132-41

[26] O'Connell, H., Chin, A., Cunnigham, C and Lawlor, B. (2004). Recent developments: Suicide in older people British Medical Journal 29 pp.895–9


**CHAPTER V**

[1] Naini, F. (2011) Facial Aesthetics: Concepts and Clinical Diagnosis. John Wiley & Sons.

[2] Naini, F. (2011) Facial Aesthetics: Concepts and Clinical Diagnosis. John Wiley & Sons. ("Figure 4.2" borrowed from text, last accessed online: 01.12.2019)

[3] Yıldız, T., & Selimen, D. (2015). The impact of facial aesthetic and reconstructive surgeries on patients' quality of life. *Indian Journal of Surgery*, *77*(3), 831-836.

[4] Barber, N. (1995). The evolutionary psychology of physical attractiveness: Sexual selection and human morphology. Ethology and Sociobiology, 16(5), 395-424.

[5] Little, A. C., Jones, B. C., & DeBruine, L. M. (2011). Facial attractiveness: evolutionary based research. Philosophical Transactions of the Royal Society B: Biological Sciences, 366(1571), 1638-1659.

[6] Langlois, J. H., Kalakanis, L., Rubenstein, A. J., Larson, A., Hallam, M., & Smoot, M. (2000). Maxims or myths of beauty? A meta-analytic and theoretical review. *Psychological bulletin*, *126*(3), 390.

[7] Sala, E., Terraneo, M., Lucchini, M., & Knies, G. (2013). Exploring the impact of male and female facial attractiveness on occupational prestige. *Research in Social Stratification and Mobility*, *31*, 69-81.

---

8 Kanazawa, S. (2011) Women are more beautiful than men. *Psychology Today.* (last accessed 06.21.2019). https://www.psychologytoday.com/intl/blog/the-scientific-fundamentalist/201101/women-are-more-beautiful-men

9 Currie, T. E., & Little, A. C. (2009). The relative importance of the face and body in judgments of human physical attractiveness. Evolution and Human Behavior, 30(6), 409–416.

10 Yancey, G., & Emerson, M. O. (2016). Does height matter? An examination of height preferences in romantic coupling. Journal of Family Issues, 37(1), 53-73.

11 Stulp, G., Buunk, A. P., Verhulst, S., & Pollet, T. V. (2015). Human height is positively related to interpersonal dominance in dyadic interactions. PloS one, 10(2), e0117860.

12 Pawlowski, B., Dunbar, R. I., & Lipowicz, A. (2000). Evolutionary fitness: tall men have more reproductive success. Nature, 403(6766), 156.

13 Nettle, D. (2002). Height and reproductive success in a cohort of British men. Human Nature, 13(4), 473-491.

14 Nettle, D. (2002). Height and reproductive success in a cohort of British men. Human Nature, 13(4), 473-491.

15 Mueller, U., & Mazur, A. (2001). Evidence of unconstrained directional selection for male tallness. Behavioral Ecology and Sociobiology, 50(4), 302-311.

16 Gladwell, M. (2006). Blink: The power of thinking without thinking.

17 Murse, Tom. (2019). Why Height and Physical Stature Play a Role in American Politics. https://www.thoughtco.com/does-the-

tallest-presidential-candidate-win-3367512 (last accessed: 10.01.2019).

[18] Stulp, G., Buunk, A. P., & Pollet, T. V. (2013). Women want taller men more than men want shorter women. Personality and Individual Differences

[19] IAT – YouTube. "S&M Short and Male Implicit Association Test Low" https://www.youtube.com/watch?v=SRlWvzUznlw - also found a preference for age and race. (last accessed 10.01.2019).

[20] Perkins, J. M., Subramanian, S. V., Davey Smith, G., & Özaltin, E. (2016). Adult height, nutrition, and population health. Nutrition reviews, 74(3), 149-165.

[21] Zhu, O. (2014) Advice in the "Love Market" from Dan Ariely. https://researchblog.duke.edu/2014/02/11/advice-in-the-love-market-from-dan-ariely/ (last accessed 01.24.2019).

[22] BBC News. (2007). Short men 'not more aggressive'". http://news.bbc.co.uk/2/hi/uk_news/6501633.stm (last accessed 05.24.2019)

[23] Morgan, J. (2018). "How to get the most right-swipes: the top 10 words to include on your dating app bio revealed" https://www.independent.co.uk/life-style/love-sex/dating-app-tinder-bio-words-most-right-swipes-music-gym-6-foot-badoo-a8512541.html (Last assessed: 03.12.2019)

[24] Provenzano, D. A., Dane, A. V., Farrell, A. H., Marini, Z. A., & Volk, A. A. (2018). Do bullies have more sex? The role of personality. *Evolutionary Psychological Science*, 4(3), 221-232.

[25] Koh, J. B., & Wong, J. S. (2017). Survival of the fittest and the sexiest: Evolutionary origins of adolescent bullying. Journal of interpersonal violence, 32(17), 2668-2690.

[26] Aromäki, A. S., Lindman, R. E., & Eriksson, C. P. (1999). Testosterone, aggressiveness, and antisocial personality. *Aggressive Behavior: Official Journal of the International Society for Research on Aggression, 25*(2), 113-123.

[27] Holzleitner, I. J., Hunter, D. W., Tiddeman, B. P., Seck, A., Re, D. E., & Perrett, D. I. (2014). Men's facial masculinity: When (body) size matters. Perception, 43(11), 1191-1202.
Klugo, R. C., & Cerny, J. C. (1978). Response of micropenis to topical testosterone and gonadotropin. The Journal of urology, 119(5), 667-668.
Mooradian, A. D., Morley, J. E., & Korenman, S. G. (1987). Biological actions of androgens. Endocrine reviews, 8(1), 1-28.

[28] Batrinos, M. L. (2012). Testosterone and aggressive behavior in man. *International journal of endocrinology and metabolism, 10*(3), 563.

[29] Carter, G. L., Campbell, A. C., & Muncer, S. (2014). The dark triad personality: Attractiveness to women. Personality and Individual Differences, 56, 57-61.

[30] Yorzinski, J. L., & Platt, M. L. (2010). Same-sex gaze attraction influences mate-choice copying in humans. PLoS One, 5(2), e9115.

[31] Eva, K. W., & Wood, T. J. (2006). Are all the taken men good? An indirect examination of mate-choice copying in humans. Cmaj, 175(12), 1573-1574.

[32] Fugère, M. A., Chabot, C., Doucette, K., & Cousins, A. J. (2017). The importance of physical attractiveness to the mate choices of women and their mothers. Evolutionary Psychological Science, 3(3), 243-252.
The researchers further "conclude that a minimum level of physical attractiveness is a necessity for both women and their mothers and that when women and their parents state that other traits are more

important than physical attractiveness, they assume potential mates meet a minimally acceptable standard of physical attractiveness." This suggests that when women claim to desire a "funny, smart, nice guy" they are being truthful, but the man needs to have met threshold of acceptable attractiveness, or his personality traits will not even be considered.

[33] Swami, V., Furnham, A., Chamorro-Premuzic, T., Akbar, K., Gordon, N., Harris, T., ... & Tovée, M. J. (2010). More than just skin deep? Personality information influences men's ratings of the attractiveness of women's body sizes. The Journal of Social Psychology, 150(6), 628-647.

[34] Holmes, L. G., & Himle, M. B. (2014). Brief report: Parent–child sexuality communication and autism spectrum disorders. Journal of autism and developmental disorders, 44(11), 2964-2970.

[35] Schöttle, D., Briken, P., Tüscher, O., & Turner, D. (2017). Sexuality in autism: hypersexual and paraphilic behavior in women and men with high-functioning autism spectrum disorder. Dialogues in clinical neuroscience, 19(4), 381.

[36] Cassidy, S., Bradley, P., Robinson, J., Allison, C., McHugh, M., & Baron-Cohen, S. (2014). Suicidal ideation and suicide plans or attempts in adults with Asperger's syndrome attending a specialist diagnostic clinic: a clinical cohort study. The Lancet Psychiatry, 1(2), 142-147.

[37] Godlasky, A. and Dastagir, A. (2018). "Suicide rate up 33% in less than 20 years, yet funding lags behind other top killers." Detroit Free Press. https://www.freep.com/in-depth/news/investigations/surviving-suicide/2018/11/28/suicide-prevention-suicidal-thoughts-research-funding/971336002/ (last accessed: 02.23.2019).

[38] Killewald, A. (2016). Money, work, and marital stability: Assessing change in the gendered determinants of divorce. American Sociological Review, 81(4), 696-719.

[39] Zagorsky, J. (2017). "Why are fewer people getting married?" https://www.pbs.org/wgbh/third-rail/episodes/episode-7-is-marriage-dead/why-are-fewer-people-getting-married/ (Last accessed: 03.01.2019).

[40] Lichter, D. T., Price, J. P., & Swigert, J. M. (2019). Mismatches in the Marriage Market. Journal of Marriage and Family.
The researchers in this project claim that there is a shortage of available men who are economically attractive, which they define as "partners with either a bachelor's degree or incomes of more than $40,000 a year."

[41] Bender, R. (2019). "Fewer people are getting married because there's a shortage of economically stable single men, says study" https://www.yahoo.com/lifestyle/fewer-people-are-getting-married-because-theres-a-shortage-of-economicallystable-single-men-says-study-221607423.html
(Last accessed: 09.22.2019)

[42] Geary, D. C., Vigil, J., & Byrd- Craven, J. (2004). Evolution of human mate choice. Journal of sex research, 41(1), 27-42. http://web.simmons.edu/~turnerg/MCC/Matechoice2PDF.pdf

[43] Hogi, F. (2014). "The 80% Approach to Dating" https://www.huffpost.com/entry/the-80-approach-to-dating_b_6165478 (Last accessed: 06.30.2019)

## CHAPTER VI

[1] Rosenfeld, M. J., Thomas, R. J., & Hausen, S. (2019). Disintermediating your friends: How online dating in the United States displaces other ways of meeting. Proceedings of the National Academy of Sciences, 116(36), 17753-17758.

[2] Data sourced from the General Social Survey (GSS), on individuals aged 22-35 who have never been married.

[3] A "Chad" is slang for a naturally good-looking man who receives a lot of positive attention from women. This could be through flirting, admiration, sex, intimacy, or a relationship.

[4] On the next page are sample conversations with a "Chadfish" named "Ray." If we are to believe these interactions, "Rays" profile biography, which includes him describing himself as being "convicted three times for rape of a child" is overlooked most likely because of his handsome face. It is important to note, that even if these interactions are truthful, any negative conversations where "Ray" is ridiculed or chastised for his profile biography were not included in the screenshot. Also, keep in mind, we do not know how often "Ray" actually matched with women or how long the account was operating in order to find matches.

Several of these "Chadfish" examples have circled the internet across different sources, so it is nearly impossible to track down the original. In this example, I was unable to track down the original "Chadfisher" responsible for this particular "Ray" account.

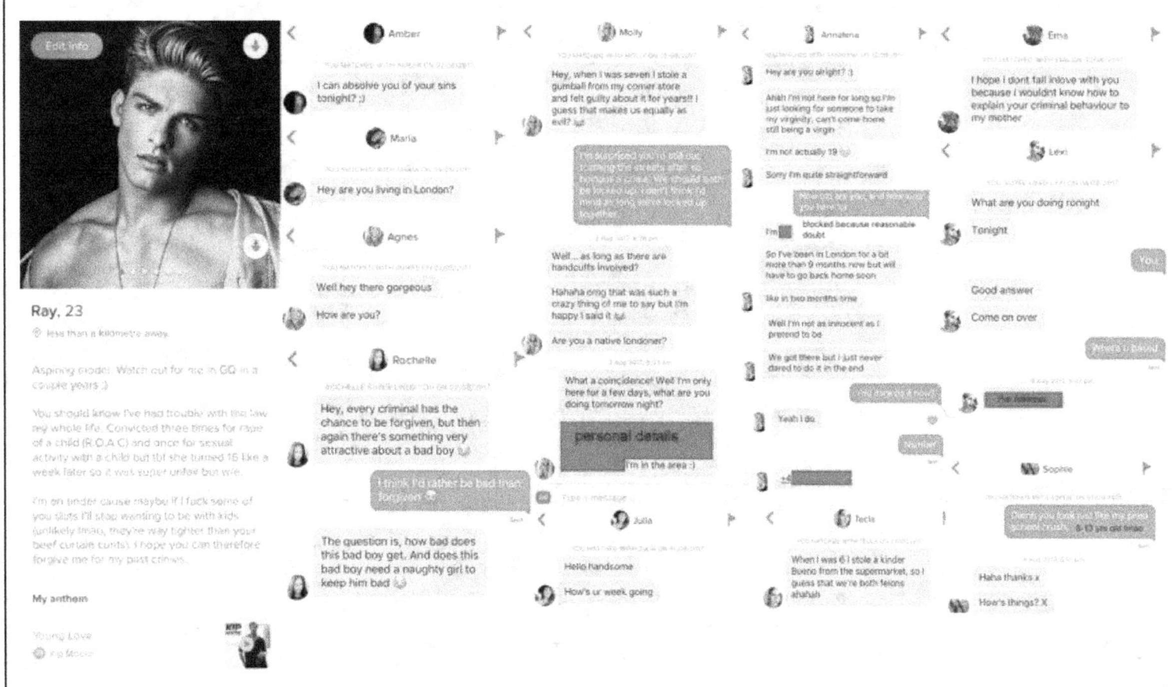

Edit info
Ray, 23
less than a kilometre away
Aspiring model. Watch out for me in GQ in a couple years :)
You should know I've had trouble with the law my whole life. Convicted three times for rape of a child (R.O.A.C) and once for sexual activity with a child but tbf she turned 16 like a week later so it was super unfair but w/e.
I'm on tinder cause maybe if I fuck some of you sluts I'll stop wanting to be with kids (unlikely tbh), they're way tighter than your beef curtain cunts\ I hope you can therefore forgive me for my past crimes.
My anthem
Young Love
Kip Moore
Amber
I can absolve you of your sins tonight? ;)
Maria
Hey are you living in London?
Agnes
Well hey there gorgeous
How are you?
Rochelle
Hey, every criminal has the chance to be forgiven, but then again there's something very attractive about a bad boy
I think I'd rather be bad than forgiven
The question is, how bad does this bad boy get. And does this bad boy need a naughty girl to keep him bad
Julia
Hello handsome
How's ur week going
Molly
Hey, when I was seven I stole a gumball from my corner store and felt guilty about it for years!! I guess that makes us equally as evil?
I'm surprised you're still out roaming the streets after so long, but's a crime. We should both be locked up, I don't think I'd mind as long some locked up together
Well... as long as there are handcuffs involved?
Hahaha omg that was such a crazy thing of me to say but I'm happy I said it
Are you a native londoner?
What a coincidence! Well I'm only here for a few days, what are you doing tomorrow night?
personal details
I'm in the area :)
Annalena
Hey are you alright? :)
Ahah I'm not here for long so I'm just looking for someone to take my virginity, can't come home still being a virgin
I'm not actually 19
Sorry I'm quite straightforward
blocked because reasonable doubt
So I've been in London for a bit more than 9 months now but will have to go back home soon
like in two months time
Well I'm not as innocent as I pretend to be
We got there but I just never dared to do it in the end
Yeah I do
Erna
I hope i dont fall inlove with you because i wouldn't know how to explain your criminal behaviour to my mother
Levi
What are you doing tonight
Tonight
Good answer
Come on over
Sophie
Haha thanks x
How's things? X
When I was 6 I stole a kinder Bueno from the supermarket, so I guess that we're both felons ahahah

5 Katz, J. E. (1997). The social side of information networking. Society, 34(3), 9-12.

6 Carpenter, C. J., & McEwan, B. (2016). The players of micro-dating: Individual and gender differences in goal orientations toward micro-dating apps. First Monday, 21(5).

7 Gatter, K., & Hodkinson, K. (2016). On the differences between Tinder™ versus online dating agencies: Questioning a myth. An exploratory study. Cogent Psychology, 3(1), 1162414.

8 Tyson, G., Perta, V. C., Haddadi, H., & Seto, M. C. (2016, August). A first look at user activity on tinder. In Proceedings of the 2016 IEEE/ACM International Conference on Advances in Social Networks Analysis and Mining (pp. 461-466). IEEE Press.

9 Tyson, G., Perta, V. C., Haddadi, H., & Seto, M. C. (2016, August). A first look at user activity on tinder. In Proceedings of the 2016 IEEE/ACM International Conference on Advances in Social Networks Analysis and Mining (pp. 461-466). IEEE Press.

10 Sumter, S. R., Vandenbosch, L., & Ligtenberg, L. (2017). Love me Tinder: Untangling emerging adults' motivations for using the dating application Tinder. Telematics and Informatics, 34(1), 67-78.

11 Wood, M. (2014). OKCupid plays with love in user experiments. The New York Times. https://www.nytimes.com/2014/07/29/technology/okcupid-publishes-findings-of-user-experiments.html (Last assessed: 03.22.2019).

12 Fugère, M. A., Chabot, C., Doucette, K., & Cousins, A. J. (2017). The importance of physical attractiveness to the mate choices of women and their mothers. Evolutionary Psychological Science, 3(3), 243-252.

## CHAPTER VII

[1] The second image is sourced from YouTube user and incel/blackpill commentator, FACEandLMS. It can found under the video entitled, "WAW5- What Makes A Jaw Attractive." His YouTube channel is: https://www.youtube.com/user/FACEandLMS (last accessed: 10.23.2019)

[2] The entire quote from Sigmund Freud, *Studies of Hysteria*, 1895: "I do not doubt that it would be easier for fate to take away your suffering than it would for me. But you will see for yourself that much has been gained if we succeed in turning your hysterical misery into common unhappiness. With a mental life that has been restored to health, you will be better armed against that unhappiness."

[3] Baumeister, R. F., & Vohs, K. D. (2004). Sexual economics: Sex as female resource for social exchange in heterosexual interactions. Personality and Social Psychology Review, 8(4), 339-363.

[4] Madhav, K. C., Sherchand, S. P., & Sherchan, S. (2017). Association between screen time and depression among US adults. Preventive medicine reports, 8, 67-71.